PRAISE FOR *50 WAYS YOU CAN HELP*

"The last election was merely a first step. We must now bring that same enthusiasm and determination to bear in order to get our country back on the right track. This book is a road map for anyone looking to make a difference."

—SENATOR RUSS FEINGOLD

"Electing Barack Obama to the presidency is the beginning of the journey, not the end. The real agenda is not to have a Democrat in the White House but to give ordinary Americans some say again. Huttner and Salzman show how we can do that."

—GOVERNOR HOWARD DEAN

"Barack Obama made public service 'cool.' *50 Ways* will help make it effective. Whatever your personal call to service, *50 Ways* has the resources you need to make a difference."

—CHRISTINE PELOSI, *Campaign Boot Camp:*
Basic Training for Future Leaders

"During his campaign, Obama empowered all of us to take part in initiating change, and it's imperative that we keep that momentum going by involving the next generation. This book is a great resource to encourage young people to embrace their civic responsibilities."

—JESSICA ALBA

"The 2008 election promised change, but achieving it means actively helping President Obama champion a progressive agenda. This book is a road map. Use it to help the president make that agenda a reality."

—DAVID SIROTA, *The Uprising: An Unauthorized Tour of the*
Populist Revolt Scaring Wall Street and Washington

"If you were one of the 69,492,376 Americans who voted for Barack Obama, your work has just begun. Huttner and Salzman envision 50 practical steps you can take to revive our economy, reclaim our environment, and renew our democracy."

—PAUL BEGALA, CNN Political Analyst

"Obama's presidency has laid the foundation for enormous change, but change is not possible without the support of the American people. This book provides a blueprint to build a cleaner, healthier, and more economically just future for all."

—PHAEDRA ELLIS-LAMKINS, CEO, Green For All

"I've witnessed the success of many of these strategies used by Huttner and Salzman in Colorado. Now they are sharing their wisdom with the entire country."

—CONGRESSMAN JARED POLIS

"One way to keep America changing and stimulate the economy is advancing the arts...and in this new era of technology, new media, and the new world of how information is shared...a new "art form" needs to be developed...This book provides simple ways to use the arts and other means for making change."

—WILL.I.AM, Black Eyed Peas

"Obama's election proved that Americans from all backgrounds can work together to defy the odds and make history. Huttner and Salzman show us how to capitalize on that first step toward reclaiming America."

—MARIA TERESA KUMAR, Executive Director, Voto Latino

50 Ways
YOU CAN HELP
OBAMA
Change America

50 Ways
YOU CAN HELP
OBAMA
Change America

MICHAEL HUTTNER
Founder of ProgressNow
&
JASON SALZMAN

POLIPOINTPRESS

13 12 11 10 09 1 2 3 4 5

Production management: BookMatters
Interior & cover design: Chris Hall/Ampersand
Cover photo: Corbis

Library of Congress Cataloging-in-Publication Data
Huttner, Michael.
  50 ways you can help Obama change America / Michael
Huttner, Jason Salzman.
      p. cm.
  ISBN 978-0-9817091-7-8 (alk. paper)
  1. Political participation—United States.   2. Politics,
Practical—United States.   3. Obama, Barack.   4. United
States—Politics and government—2009-
I. Salzman, Jason.   II. Title.   III. Title: Fifty ways you can
help Obama change America.
  JK1764.H886 2009
  323'.0420973—dc22   2009024669

Published by:
PoliPointPress, LLC
80 Liberty Ship Way, Suite 22
Sausalito, CA 94965
(415) 339-4100
www.p3books.com

Distributed by Ingram Publisher Services

Printed in the USA

This victory alone is not the change we seek—it is only the chance for us to make that change. And that cannot happen if we go back to the way things were. It cannot happen without you.

—President-elect Barack Obama, election night victory speech, November 4, 2008, Grant Park, Chicago, IL

Contents

Introduction — *xiii*

Turn Obama's Vision into Law — 1

1. Achieve Energy Independence — 3
2. Help Fix the Health-Care Mess — 7
3. Straighten Out Federal Budget Priorities — 11
4. Clean Up Campaign Financing — 17
5. Level the Playing Field for Working Families — 22
6. Protect the Openness of the Internet — 26
7. Sign Up for President Obama's E-mail List — 29

Become a Community Organizer — 35

8. Reach Out to Diverse Constituencies — 37
9. Attend a Leadership Training — 42
10. Build a Neighborhood Team — 47
11. Call, Write, E-mail, or Meet Lawmakers — 51
12. Throw a House Party for Change — 56
13. Testify at a Public Hearing or Meeting — 61
14. Get a Job to Help Change America — 66
15. Support Political Art — 70

16. Open Doors for Young People · 74

17. Organize Your Place of Worship · 77

Volunteer in Your Community · 81

18. Respond to Obama's Call for National Service · 83

19. Help the Homeless · 87

20. Assist Your Local Library · 90

21. Support Our Troops and Veterans · 93

22. Volunteer at a School · 97

23. Spread Change Worldwide · 101

Be the Change · 105

24. Rescue a Pound Puppy! · 107

25. Inspire Yourself to Stay Involved · 110

26. Plant Your Own Garden · 113

27. Get News That's Truly Fair and Balanced · 117

28. Use Public Transportation · 121

29. Support Socially Responsible Businesses · 124

30. Green Your Home for the Earth's Sake · 128

31. Spend More Time with Your Kids · 132

32. Quit Smoking · 136

Amplify Your Voice for Change · 141

33. Take Back the Flag · 143

34. Make a Statement on the Streets · 147

35. Stage or Attend a Rally, Media Event, or Protest · 151

36. Hold Extremists Accountable 157

37. Feed a Story to a Columnist or Blogger 162

38. Support Obama in a Letter to the Editor
or Online Comment 166

39. Reach Out to Conservatives 170

Harness the New Media 177

40. Use Your Cell Phone and Text Messages for Change 179

41. Be a Media Watchdog and Challenge Journalists 183

42. Make a YouTube Video 187

43. Pass on Online Action Alerts 191

44. Social Network for Obama 195

Act Now to Win Future Elections 201

45. Help the Census Count Everybody 203

46. Become a Precinct Captain 208

47. Run for Local Office 212

48. Volunteer on a Campaign 216

49. Register New Voters Year-Round 220

50. Donate to Causes You Believe In 225

Conclusion 229

Share Your Ideas to Help Obama Change America 231

Acknowledgments 235

About the Authors 237

About ProgressNow 238

To Debbie and Anne, our parents, our children, and each of you who are working to make America a better place.

—MH & JS

Introduction

Starting today, we must pick ourselves up, dust ourselves off, and begin again the work of remaking America.

—*President Barack Obama, inaugural speech,*
January 20, 2009, Washington DC

IN MANY WAYS, it seemed like a miracle. We elected Barack Obama President of the United States. We volunteered for him, voted for him, and were so overwhelmed and inspired by his victory that we had tears in our eyes on election night.

But what do we do now? How can we help President Obama actually change America?

This book answers that question. We've compiled 50 ways you can help Obama change our country. This book explains what you can do from home, in your community, across our country, and around the world.

Each of the actions suggested here is connected to something President Obama advocated as part of his campaign for change—or to something he said or did himself during his life as a community organizer, a politician, and even as a father and husband. All of our chapters begin with a quote from the president that touches on the recommended action. So our suggestions on how to support Obama reflect the ways Obama himself has taken action over the course of his life to advance the cause of change.

There's lots of work to be done to clean up President Bush's eight years in office. And President Obama can't do it without our help, just like he couldn't have gotten elected without a flood of support from people who believed in him.

The uprising can't stop now. Republicans, Democrats, and independents alike believe in Obama and approve of the job he's doing. Lots of people want to help him but don't know how. We don't pretend to have all the answers, but this book is a place to start.

Our 50 suggestions cover seven themes:

- **Turn Obama's Vision into Law.** This explains how you can help advance President Obama's proposals for energy independence, universal health care, campaign finance reform, and more.

- **Become a Community Organizer.** Learn how to do what our community-organizer-in-chief did as a young man and during his campaigns—and mobilize your community to support change.

- **Volunteer in Your Community.** Find out how to respond to President Obama's call for community service in your area and around the world.

- **Be the Change.** Here are ways you can adjust your own life, at home or on a personal level, to reflect President Obama's vision.

- **Amplify Your Voice for Change.** Agreeing with the folks around your kitchen table is fine, but here you can find out how to communicate to a wider audience to help make change a reality.

- **Harness the New Media.** Use the latest tactics on behalf of President Obama's agenda and change in your community.

- **Act Now to Win Future Elections.** This section includes ideas for how to sustain change in America and nurture the success of Obama-like candidates at all levels.

In addition to practical information and tips for action, you'll find stories from the front lines, where people are fighting to keep President Obama's momentum going. You'll read about people who powered President Obama's success—and then found a way to do more.

This book is written for those of us who *still* want to do more. No matter which actions you choose, whether you have the time to organize a rally or simply to click a mouse, all our efforts make a difference. It's up to us, collectively, to make the world a better place, not just talk about it. Or assume President Obama will do it for us.

As President Obama said, the work we have in front of us is even more challenging than winning the election in the first place.

We know it's not easy to dust ourselves off and get going on a task as gigantic as remaking America, but we can't stop now. We can't let this opportunity for change pass us by.

Turn Obama's Vision into Law

My attitude about something like the presidency is that you don't want to just be the president. You want to change the country.

—*Senator Barack Obama, "Path to Power,"*
Men's Vogue, *September 2006*

[1]

Achieve Energy Independence

At a time when our ice caps are melting and our oceans are rising, we need you to help lead a green revolution. We still have time to avoid the catastrophic consequences of climate change if we get serious about investing in renewable sources of energy; and if we get a generation of volunteers to work on renewable energy projects, and teach folks about conservation, and help clean up polluted areas; and if we send talented engineers and scientists abroad to help developing countries promote clean energy.

—*Senator Barack Obama,*
Wesleyan University Commencement,
May 25, 2008, Middletown, CT

THE CHALLENGE

Since just about everything we use—from toasters and alarm clocks in the morning to automobiles and stereos at night—is powered by fossil fuels, it's obvious that finding alternative sources of energy is essential to our national security.

That's why President Obama wants it to be on the nation's front burner, so to speak.

But "energy independence" does not simply mean reducing oil imports from the Middle East or elsewhere and continuing our dependence on fossil fuels obtained from our own territory. It means using renewable energy sources and energy-efficient technologies that will reduce or eliminate our need for fossil fuels.

There's no doubt that making America energy independent would go a long way toward enhancing our national security (think: no more wars over oil), preserving the environment (less emission of global-warming gases), ramping up the economy (to be more competitive), and more. And President Obama has articulated the need for energy independence, recognizing the realistic limits on how fast clean energy technology can be further developed and deployed.

PRACTICAL INFORMATION

- An investment of $100 billion in clean energy would create three times as many good jobs as the same investment in the oil industry.

- Each of the years from 1998 to 2008 ranked among the top 25 warmest years ever recorded.

- The thickness of the Arctic ice cap has decreased by 40 percent since the 1960s.

- Americans consume 21 million barrels of oil each day, and about 70 percent of it is used on transportation.

  (Sources: Center for American Progress, National Oceanic and Atmospheric Administration, NASA, National Commission on Energy Policy)

WHAT *YOU* CAN DO

Green your home. See our chapter, "Green Your Home for the Earth's Sake."

Green your car. President Obama pledged to put one million plug-in hybrid cars—cars that can get up to 150 miles per gallon—on the road by 2015. Consider getting one.

Join a clean energy organization and track the energy debate in Congress. President Obama has assembled a top-notch team to fight for clean energy and against climate change. Members of Congress are lending support by taking leadership roles against fossil-fuel interests and their front groups. The battle is shifting by the day, so we advise you to join the e-mail list of a few of the groups listed in the recommended resources section. Once you begin getting their e-mails, you can decide which group or groups you want to pursue.

Pay particularly close attention to centrist "Blue Dog" Democrats in Congress. Led by Senator Evan Bayh of Indiana, these senators are key to moving Obama's climate and energy reform agenda forward, as are energy committee members like Senator Lisa Murkowski of Alaska, who is the ranking Republican.

RECOMMENDED RESOURCES

The Alliance for Climate Protection, www.climateprotect.org, chaired by Al Gore, looks to show the American people—and people elsewhere in the world—the importance and urgency of adopting and implementing effective and comprehensive solutions for the climate crisis. Gore's Web site for *An Inconvenient Truth,* www.climatecrisis.net, provides practical steps you can take to reduce your impact on the Earth.

Apollo Alliance, www.apolloalliance.org, advocates a "new Apollo program" for America that will wean us from oil—just as John Kennedy's program succeeded in landing a person on the moon in the 1960s.

Energy Action Coalition, www.energyactioncoalition.org, focuses on mobilizing students and youth in support of clean energy and climate legislation.

Green for All, www.greenforall.org, founded by Van Jones, whom President Obama appointed as special White House Advisor for "green jobs," is an organization dedicated to building a green and just economy.

League of Conservation Voters, www.lcv.org, focuses on the U.S. Congress— information on proposed legislation, how senators and representatives voted on environmental issues, and pre-election evaluations of candidates.

Pickens Plan, www.pickensplan.com, is the brainchild of Texas oilman T. Boone Pickens, who is organizing groups to pass elements of his "Pickens Plan," which includes steps toward energy independence, in every congressional district in America.

Sierra Club, www.sierraclub.org/energy, is a well-respected national organization with state chapters that focus on energy and climate issues.

Union of Concerned Scientists, www.ucsusa.org/action, offers an updated menu of ways to help pass meaningful energy and climate legislation.

[2]

Help Fix the Health-Care Mess

I want to wake up and know that every single American has health care when they need it, that every senior has prescription drugs they can afford, and that no parents are going to bed at night worrying about how they'll afford medicine for a sick child. That's the future we can build together.

—*Senator Barack Obama,*
Town Hall, June 5, 2008, Bristol, VA

THE CHALLENGE

Our country's ailing health-care system is not only potentially disastrous for the millions of Americans who lack insurance, but it also puts our nation's economy at a competitive disadvantage due, in part, to the increased costs incurred by U.S. companies.

That's why more businesses in our country are standing up, along with the uninsured and those who are inadequately covered, and demanding health-care reform. It makes no sense that the United States, the world's richest nation, has such an inadequate health-care system, especially when Americans spend twice as much as other industrialized nations on health care.

As a first step toward addressing this problem, Obama guided a bill through Congress giving health insurance to millions of kids. Even with the narrow focus on vulnerable kids, whose health-care needs are obvious, passage of this bill in Congress was by no means a certainty. In the Senate, 32 votes were cast against it.

Now Obama faces the daunting task of steering broader health-care reform measures through Congress. Hillary Clinton famously tried and failed to lead such reforms, because the voices of special interests were heard more loudly in Congress than the people's voices. This time it's essential for Congress to prioritize the public interest over special interests. But you can be sure this won't happen without serious organizational efforts on our part.

President Obama is ready to move forward. As he stated in his first address to a joint session of Congress: "Health-care reform cannot wait, it must not wait, and it will not wait another year."

Experts—and common sense—tell us that one of the best investments we can make for our own people is to make sure they have access to first-class health care.

FROM THE FRONT LINES

> Health-care reform is coming. Cash-strapped consumers are clamoring for it. Business owners small and large demand it because they know our economy needs it. Even the insurance and pharmaceutical industries expect it. If ever there was a time for all of us to weigh in, it's now.
>
> —*Jeff Blum, Executive Director, USAction*

PRACTICAL INFORMATION

- Ninety percent of Americans say the health-care system needs to be changed fundamentally. One in four families said they had a problem paying for insurance in the past year—and two-thirds of those families had insurance.

- Over 45 million Americans lack health insurance—and that number is projected to rise to 56 million by 2013 unless reforms are enacted.

- Since 2000, about five million families declared bankruptcy because they couldn't pay their health-care bills after a medical crisis.

(Sources: AFL-CIO, Center for American Progress)

WHAT *YOU* CAN DO

Clarify your own position on health-care reform, and join an organization that promotes your preferred approach. Progressive organizations have different solutions to America's health-care problems. Some are more aligned with Obama's approach, which alters the basic structure of the current system to extend coverage to many more Americans, while others favor a "single-payer" system, in which the federal government becomes the insurance carrier for all Americans. In the following section of recommended resources, you'll find organizations advocating both positions.

RECOMMENDED RESOURCES

American Health Care Reform, www.americanhealthcarereform.org, provides state-by-state health-care information with a focus on a single-payer national health insurance approach.

Families USA, www.familiesusa.org, is a national nonprofit, nonpartisan organization dedicated to the achievement of high-quality, affordable health care for all Americans. Working at the national, state, and community levels, this organization has earned a national reputation as an effective voice for health-care consumers for 25 years.

Health Care for America Now (HCAN), www.healthcareforamericanow.org, is a grassroots network that includes labor organizations, MoveOn .org, the NAACP, USAction, and many others, and is dedicated to winning quality, affordable health care. Its Web site tracks the legislative action on health care in Congress and targets specific lawmakers who will be making key votes on upcoming legislation. The HCAN Web site lays out a step-by-step plan to move health-care reform through Congress.

Physicians for a National Health Program, www.pnhp.org, is an organization that backs a Canadian-style single-payer health-care system, under which all U.S. citizens would automatically receive health insurance through a program run by the federal government. It suggests actions to move national health insurance forward.

[3]

Straighten Out
Federal Budget Priorities

Now, there are those who say the plans in this budget are too ambitious to enact; to say that—they say that in the face of challenges that we face, we should be trying to do less, [rather] than more. What I say is that the challenges we face are too large to ignore. The cost of our health care is too high to ignore. The dependence on oil is too dangerous to ignore. Our education deficit is growing too wide to ignore. To kick these problems down the road for another four years or another eight years would be to continue the same irresponsibility that led us to this point. That's not why I ran for this office. I didn't come here to pass on our problems to the next President or the next generation—I came here to solve them.

—President Barack Obama,
statement by the president on the budget,
The White House, March 17, 2009, Washington DC

THE CHALLENGE

The federal budget is where most of Obama's vision hits reality. The attacks on the president by people like Dick Cheney don't matter in the end. But getting enough votes in Congress to pass Obama's programs does.

Most of the debate in Congress centers on the budget: whether to spend more money on renewable energy, like wind turbines and solar power, and less money on Cold War weapons, like the F-22 fighter jet; or whether to cut taxes for the middle class and raise them for the rich; or whether to increase humanitarian foreign aid or continue spending over $100 billion annually in Iraq.

The federal budget is central to all the issues we care about. It's the heart of what we elected Obama to change, because federal spending priorities, as author Jim Wallis and others have noted, reflect the core values of our country.

PRACTICAL INFORMATION

- The Congress doesn't have an "up or down vote" on the entire budget. Slices of it are debated and approved, altered, or rejected in different committees and then in the full House and Senate. Ultimately, the budget is divided up into major pieces of legislation, which are voted on by both houses of Congress. Then the president signs or vetoes them.

- Many of the most significant policy initiatives and changes to federal spending on different programs are offered as amendments to budget legislation. Some stand-alone bills are passed by Congress, and some are extremely important, but budget legislation is the major focus for Congress.

- About 59 percent of the discretionary budget—the money Congress votes to spend each year—goes to the military versus 2 percent for science, 4 percent for international affairs, and 7 percent for education.

(Source: National Priorities Project)

WHAT *YOU* CAN DO

Sign up for Organizing for America. The most important budget actions will be spotlighted by this group, which is an extension of Obama's election campaign organization. Many of its suggested actions going forward will focus directly on passing elements of the federal budget—or fighting extreme-right-wing campaigns to defeat them.

Try joining a few DC-based groups that follow the issues you care most about as they are debated during the congressional budget process. In separate chapters, we spotlight groups that are mobilizing citizens to support congressional actions relating to energy, health care, Internet, campaign finance, and labor issues. Below are groups that monitor other issues and suggest ways citizens can make a difference. It's unrealistic to track all of it, but you can follow some of it by signing up to receive alerts from these nonpartisan citizen groups:

Children

- Children's Defense Fund, www.childrensdefense.org, promotes a variety of children's issues.

Civil Rights

- American Civil Liberties Union, www.aclu.org, follows national developments.
- Amnesty International, www.amnestyusa.org, is an organization that promotes international and national human rights.

Education

- National Education Association, www.nea.org, deals with public education issues.

Environmental Issues

- League of Conservation Voters, www.lcv.org, tracks proposed legislation, how senators and representatives voted on environmental issues, and pre-election evaluations.
- Natural Resources Defense Council, www.nrdc.org, tracks many issues in Congress.
- Sierra Club, www.sierraclub.org, focuses on environmental issues.

International Aid

- Bread for the World, www.bread.org, is a collective whose mission is to end world hunger.

Military Spending

- Center for Defense Information, www.cdi.org, covers military spending issues.
- Council for a Livable World, www.clw.org, focuses on nuclear weapons.

Poverty and Housing

- USAction, www.usaction.org, builds progressive coalitions by organizing issue and election campaigns to improve people's lives, especially in low-income and diverse communities.

Tax Policy

- United for a Fair Economy, www.faireconomy.org, focuses on the estate tax.

- Tax Policy Center, www.taxpolicycenter.org, provides analysis and facts about tax policy.

Women's Issues

- NARAL Pro-choice America, www.naral.org, is a national advocate for reproductive rights.

- The National Organization for Women, www.now.org, is a feminist advocacy group.

- Planned Parenthood Federation of America, www. plannedparenthood.org, provides health care and sex education, and advocates reproductive rights.

RECOMMENDED RESOURCES

Campaign to Rebuild and Renew America Now, www.rebuildandrenew.org, is a coalition of groups that have formed specifically to encourage citizens to take action to pass the president's budget. This is an easy place to find ways to take action!

Center for American Progress, www.americanprogress.org, tracks multiple federal budget issues, many discussed in a free newsletter.

Center on Budget and Policy Priorities, www.centeronbudget.org, provides in-depth analysis of federal spending on numerous issues.

Common Dreams, www.commondreams.org/progressive-community, is a list of progressive groups, many with a presence in Washington DC.

Consumers Union, www.consumerunion.org is an expert, independent, nonprofit organization whose mission is to work for a fair, just, and safe marketplace for all consumers and to empower consumers to protect themselves.

National Priorities Project, www.nationalpriorities.org, demonstrates how the federal budget is currently allocated among competing priorities (e.g., education versus defense) and what could be done if the federal budget were spent in different ways.

Progressive States Network, www.progressivestates.org, aims to transform the political landscape by sparking progressive actions on budget and other policy issues at the state level.

Women's Action for New Directions, www.wand.org/csba/fedbudget.pdf, is a great primer on the federal budget process.

[4]

Clean Up Campaign Financing

There are technical fixes to our democracy that might relieve some of this pressure on politicians, structural changes that would strengthen the link between voters and their representatives. Nonpartisan districting, same-day registration, and weekend elections would all increase the competitiveness of races and might spur more participation from the electorate—and the more the electorate is paying attention, the more integrity is rewarded. Public financing of campaigns or free television and radio time could drastically reduce the constant scrounging for money and the influence of special interests.

—*Senator Barack Obama, "Politics,"* The Audacity of Hope

THE CHALLENGE

President Barack Obama understands the need for campaign finance reform. In fact, one of his first victories as a state legislator was moving a campaign finance reform bill through the Illinois Legislature, prohibiting his colleagues from raising campaign funds on state property or taking gifts from lobbyists and special interest groups. And one of his first actions as president was to ban his staff from accepting gifts from lobbyists and to restrict his staff from lobbying after they leave their posts, among other things.

Now we should help the president champion even more meaningful campaign finance reform: public financing for election campaigns.

Some argue that America should give up on regulating campaign funds because money in politics is like water: it flows around obstacles that get in its way. But people build dams and direct streams. And we can also control the flow of money to politicians if we want to build the barriers into our campaign system.

The argument for doing so is irrefutable. Public officials spend as much as half their time raising money, leaving them captives of wealthy donors. That's because they hear more from the donor class than any other group of people. Time constraints preclude even the most conscientious politicians from doing otherwise. And just the prospect of spending so much time fund-raising keeps talented people from becoming politicians.

Candidates spend huge chunks of their campaign dollars on advertising. So meaningful campaign finance reform needs to include public funding of candidate communications.

Some people think there's no way to clean up this corrosive effect of money in politics. But we've actually got the solution. What we don't have is the political will of incumbents to enact meaningful reform. That's where you come in, by calling on your elected representatives to endorse the full public financing of election campaigns.

FROM THE FRONT LINES

At the federal level, we need to wipe the slate clean by replacing existing laws with a robust system of public financing and full disclosure of all campaign activities, including issue advertising and voter education.

We should not conflate the lobbying activities of those who seek to advance their economic interests with the lobbying activities of those who are promoting the public interest or an ideological position. There's a difference between those who are trying to secure earmarks for their company and those trying, for example, to secure benefits for the disabled.

—*Michael Vachon, advisor to
the chairman of Soros Fund Management*

PRACTICAL INFORMATION

- Seven states and two cities have enacted clean election laws: Arizona; Connecticut; Maine; New Jersey; New Mexico; North Carolina; Vermont; Albuquerque, New Mexico; and Portland, Oregon. Find out about campaign finance reform organizing in your state by clicking on the home page of www.publiccampaign.org or www.commoncause.org.

- Over 2.5 million people contributed over $300 million to Barack Obama's election campaign in donations of $400 or less.

WHAT *YOU* CAN DO

Ask your representatives to support the Fair Elections Now Act. Introduced in both houses of Congress, this bill would allow federal candidates to seek office without relying on big donors. Candidates would qualify for federal funding by raising small donations in their home states. Qualifying candidates would receive discounts and vouchers for TV advertising—and receive extra funding to offset the advantage of a self-financed opponent. The cost of public financing under this bill would be covered by a small fee on large government contractors.

Sample letter to your senators and representatives (provided by Common Cause):

Dear XXX:

I strongly urge you to support the Fair Elections Now Act aimed at curbing the influence of wealthy donors and lobbyists in Washington.

The bipartisan bill would create a full voluntary system of public funding for congressional candidates. Candidates able to show a threshold level of public support by collecting qualifying contributions of $5 from a set number of voters in their state and who are willing to forego further private contributions can qualify for public funding to run a competitive campaign.

With the corrupting role of big money in politics on display in recent congressional scandals and as campaign costs skyrocket, it's clear that we need a system that encourages candidates and lawmakers to respond to the will of the voters, not to further cozy up to wealthy donors and special interests. The Fair Elections Now Act features an opt-in full public financing system.

Support the Fair Elections Now Act and help ensure that qualified candidates with good ideas are able to seek positions of leadership; that all candidates are able to spend their time on the campaign trail listening to constituents, rather than going after contributions; and that elected officials will be free to focus on the challenges facing our nation, rather than making nice with donors.

It's only fair. Support the Fair Elections Now Act and ask your colleagues to do the same.

RECOMMENDED RESOURCES

Brennan Center for Justice, www.brennancenter.org, is an excellent source for research and policy on campaign finance reform.

Common Cause, www.commoncause.org, promotes government ethics, fair elections, media reform, and public campaign financing, among other issues.

Public Campaign Action Fund, www.campaignmoney.org, advocates sweeping campaign finance reform at both the state and federal level, including publicly financed elections.

[5]

Level the Playing Field
for Working Families

We're ready to play offense for organized labor. It's time we had a president who didn't choke saying the word "union." A president who knows it's the Department of Labor and not the Department of Management. And a president who strengthens our unions by letting them do what they do best—organize our workers. If a majority of workers want a union, they should get a union. It's that simple. Let's stand up to the business lobby that's been getting their friends in Washington to block card check. I've fought to pass the Employee Free Choice Act in the Senate. And I will make it the law of the land when I'm President of the United States of America.

—*Senator Barack Obama,*
remarks to AFL-CIO,
April 2, 2008, in Philadelphia, PA

THE CHALLENGE

Barack Obama wants to give workers a stronger voice in America. And one of the best ways to accomplish this is to make it easier for them to form unions. Workers who want union representation today are routinely harassed by employers, and their efforts to form unions are often derailed or delayed to death.

So it's not surprising that the top priority of America's labor leaders is the passage of a law that would level the playing field for American workers when it comes to forming unions in the workplace. The proposed law to accomplish this is the Employee Free Choice Act, which would allow workers to vote to form unions by signing a card. In the past, employers could mandate that workers vote in secret to form a union, but this system was unfair. It allowed employers to intimidate and propagandize workers who might be required, among other things, to attend meetings with employers about the union drive. Union organizers, on the other hand, could not call mandatory meetings with fellow employees.

Once a majority of workers sign up, the act requires the designated union and the company involved to negotiate a contract within 120 days. If no agreement is reached, binding arbitration is required as a last resort. In the past, employers could delay this negotiating process indefinitely or refuse to agree to a contract at all.

The Employee Free Choice Act gives workers a chance to fight back against giant corporations that are exploiting them, as CEOs bring home massive paychecks while the working families struggle to pay for the basics.

PRACTICAL INFORMATION

- Over half of employers, when faced with a union-organizing drive, threaten to close their workplaces if employees form a union, and a quarter of employers fire at least one pro-union worker.

- Surveys indicate that over a third of workers vote against unions due to pressure from their employers.

- Unionized workers earn up to 30 percent more than non-unionized workers.

- More than half of America's workers say they would join a union if they could.

- Cingular Wireless and Kaiser Permanente are two corporations that have already shown success using the tenets of the Employee Free Choice Act in dealings with their workers.

(Source: American Rights at Work)

FROM THE FRONT LINES

Enacting the Employee Free Choice Act is the single most important and effective economic recovery plan to ensure that America's middle class is rebuilt through higher wages, better health care and more secure pensions. This legislation gives workers more choice and levels the playing field by allowing them to form a union without management's interference or intimidation by imposing strict penalties on employers who break the law and violate their employees' right to organize.

—Anna Burger, secretary-treasurer
of the Service Employees International Union

WHAT *YOU* CAN DO

Obama has been a strong supporter of the Employee Free Choice Act, and it's likely he'll sign the bill if it can get through Congress. The House passed the act last year, and it will probably do so again. So the focus now is to pressure the U.S. Senate to pass the act. Here's what you can do:

Determine who your senators are, if you need to. Go to http://senate.gov and click on "Senators."

Write a letter (handwritten preferred) to your senator asking him or her to support the Employee Free Choice Act. Send to: Senator_____, U.S. Senate, Washington DC, 20510.

Send a thank-you note to President Barack Obama for his support of the Employee Free Choice Act. Send to: President Barack Obama, The White House, 1600 Pennsylvania Ave, NW, Washington DC, 20500.

Visit the Web site of American Rights at Work (listed in the recommended resources section) for campaign updates and timely actions. And sign their online petition in support of the Employee Free Choice Act.

RECOMMENDED RESOURCES

AFL-CIO, www.aflcio.org, is a federation of dozens of unions. For grassroots actions, visit www.workingamerica.org.

American Rights at Work, www.americanrightsatwork.org, promotes the rights of workers to join unions.

Service Employees International Union, www.seiu.org, is the largest union in America, organizing grassroots activities in part through www.changetowin.org.

[6]

Protect the Openness of the Internet

To seize this moment, we have to ensure free and full exchange of information, and that starts with an open Internet. I will take a back seat to no one in my commitment to network neutrality, because once providers start to privilege some applications or Web sites over others, then the smaller voices get squeezed out and we all lose. The Internet is perhaps the most open network in history, and we have to keep it that way.

—Senator Barack Obama,
Google Headquarters,
November 14, 2007, Mountain View, CA

THE CHALLENGE

President Obama's own election campaign is proof of why we should keep the Internet open. His campaign inspired a flood of voices and creativity on the Web—from YouTube videos and Facebook groups to poems and art—unlike anything we've seen anywhere ever.

The Internet worked for Obama, as it works for grassroots activists, artists, entrepreneurs, writers, and the like, because it treats everyone equally. So, for example, during the last election, the video we sent to our friends of our Obama-crazed kids selling lemonade and chanting

"Lemonade for change" traveled just as fast across the Internet as Honda's video advertising the new Accord. Thank goodness for that.

But big phone and cable companies want to change access to the Internet. Currently these "Internet providers" carry data. That's it. They don't decide that certain data (videos, imagery, sound, anything) from one Web site, like Honda's, will move faster across the Web than data from another Web site, like yours.

Now these phone and cable companies want to charge fees to guarantee fast delivery. This would mean that some people and companies would have a "fast lane" on the Web, while others would be relegated to the back roads.

So instead of the Internet that we're used to, where data from all sources travels at equal speeds, they want to discriminate, speeding up delivery for those who pay more and slowing it down or stopping it for those who can't.

PRACTICAL INFORMATION

- Preserving the openness of the Internet is also called "network neutrality" or "net neutrality." Currently the companies that carry Internet data are neutral—they don't send a giant corporation's data any faster than anyone else's. But if net neutrality is lost, Internet providers could allow some data to move faster than other data.

- Net neutrality is favored by a wide coalition of organizations, from the Christian Coalition and the Consumer's Union to PETA and Free Press and beyond. This isn't a left versus right issue at all.

- The current system of non-discriminatory or neutral access to the Internet has been in place since the Internet was created.

WHAT *YOU* CAN DO

Sign the "Save the Internet" petition and spread the word. Find it at: www.savetheinternet.com. You can receive updates and information on recruiting organizations, creating a web banner, and informing your friends about the campaign to preserve net neutrality.

Write or call your members of Congress. Ask them to protect net neutrality. Use the information from the organizations listed in the recommended resources section.

FROM THE FRONT LINES

Fast, affordable, neutral Internet is the lifeblood of the grassroots politics that swept Barack Obama into office. We best pay close attention to the policy decisions that are shaping the future of the Net, or the largest communications companies will seize control, and future campaigns like Obama's will stand no chance of victory.

—Josh Silver, executive director of Free Press

RECOMMENDED RESOURCES

The Center for Public Integrity, http://projects.publicintegrity.org/telecom, tracks media owners and telecommunications policy.

Free Press, www.freepress.net, is a national media-reform organization with multiple campaigns and lots of information.

Save the Internet, www.savetheinternet.com, is a broad coalition of groups supporting net neutrality.

[7]

Sign Up for President Obama's E-mail List

The movement you built is too important to stop growing now. Today I am pleased to announce the creation of Organizing for America, the organization that will build on the movement you started during the campaign. As president, I will need the help of all Americans to meet the challenges that lie ahead. That's why I am asking people like you, who fought for change during the campaign, to continue fighting for change in your communities.

—President-elect Barack Obama,
January 18, 2009, in an e-mail to 13 million supporters

THE CHALLENGE

Our country's community-organizer-in-chief, President Barack Obama, would definitely agree that people need to come together to make change happen. For the small task we have in front of us now—fundamental change in America—the need to work together for common goals is huge. There's just no other way to go.

So, whether your primary concern is education, the environment, the economy, or some other issue, try to do what President Obama suggests needs to be done, rather than pushing for stuff that's not on his agenda. Notice we wrote the word "try." We know Obama is not perfect, and some of the compromises he has to make are hard to swallow. But if ever there was a time to stretch as far as you can go to support him, it's now.

The best way to do this, and perhaps the single most important suggestion in this entire book, is to join the e-mail list of President Obama's group: Organizing for America. Each week or so, you'll get an e-mail explaining what Obama's team thinks is the most important way for you to help move the president's agenda forward. All of us, to maximize our coordinated power, should try hard to take the recommended actions and to work together to advance progressive goals.

Organizing for America grew out of President Obama's election campaign. All those people who signed up to help during the election are now on his list to continue to press for change. Since Election Day, cynics have been saying that there's no way President Obama can mobilize his campaign supporters on behalf of his presidential agenda. The way to prove the cynics wrong is to sign up for Organizing for America and take action.

Here's a sample e-mail from Organizing for America, asking us to help Obama with his first Supreme Court nominee:

> This week, hundreds of thousands of supporters like you stood up to support Judge Sonia Sotomayor's historic nomination to the U.S. Supreme Court. But the long road to confirmation has only just begun. Add your voice, and stand with Sotomayor.
>
> We've just launched our action center, an online hub where you can find all the tools you need to help spread the word about Judge Sotomayor, engage in the public debate about her nomination, and make sure decision-makers in the Senate know where you stand. With only a few minutes, you can make a huge difference.
>
> Check out the action center and help confirm this great nominee.
>
> In the coming days and weeks, our opponents will try to play politics with Judge Sotomayor's nomination, and it's up to us to help

get out the facts and show the public—and key decision-makers—how much support she really has. Here's how you can help:

- **Stand with Sotomayor**—You can add your name to our public display of support, showing the Senate and the media where the American people stand.

- **Write a letter to the editor**—Using our easy online tool, you can send a letter to your local newspaper about why you support Judge Sotomayor's nomination—highlighting her extraordinary life story, her tremendous judicial experience, the historic nature of her nomination, or anything else that's important to you. It's extremely effective and only takes a few minutes.

- **Call your senator**—You can look up the numbers of your two senators, and give them a call to let them know that you support Judge Sotomayor and hope they do too.

- **Share President Obama's message**—The president has recorded a special message explaining his support for Judge Sotomayor— you can send it on to help educate friends and family.

- **Display your support**—Download posters and get images you can use online to show your support.

Whichever actions you take, you'll be playing a critical role in this historic moment.

Please visit the action center now.

http://my.barackobama.com/courtactioncenter

Thank you,

Mitch

Mitch Stewart

Director, Organizing for America

PRACTICAL INFORMATION

E-mails from Organizing for America will suggest many of the types of actions we outline in the book, like hosting a house party or calling and meeting with elected officials. Most of the time, all you do is click your mouse, and you'll get all the information you need to participate in the suggested action. Or you might be asked to pick up the phone and call your congressional representatives, using the phone numbers provided.

Organizing for America has 14 million names on its e-mail list. Its goal is to have at least one full-time paid staffer in all states, with more employees in key states.

WHAT *YOU* CAN DO

Create an account at www.my.barackobama.com. Fill out the information under "Create an Account." You're done! (It's worth perusing the Web site for a while, checking out the blog and the stuff you can do, but signing up is the first and most important step.)

Read the e-mails! If nothing else, at least read the e-mails from President Obama's organization. Don't just delete them. You may be more inspired than you think. (We're not big on authority, but he is the closest thing to our president that we've seen in our lifetimes. We can show him some respect by reading his group's e-mails.)

Request that your friends forward the e-mails. Tell your friends what we wrote above and ask them to forward the e-mails from Organizing for America.

Share Organizing for America's e-mails. Even if you know your friends also get President Obama's e-mails, forward them anyway, particularly the ones that strike you as the most important. If your friends are busy and perhaps deleting the President's e-mails (gasp), your forwarded e-mail may get their attention.

Tell people who may not be signed up for Organizing for America. All of us know a few people who might not be signed up for Organizing for America—or might have dropped it after the campaign. Make a special effort, not just by forwarding them an e-mail but by calling them as well, to get them to sign up.

RECOMMENDED RESOURCES

Organizing for America, www.my.barackobama.com, is President Obama's campaign Web site, transformed to organize citizens for progressive change. Sign up!

Become a Community Organizer

I was a young organizer then, intent on fighting joblessness and poverty on the South Side, and I still remember one of the very first meetings I put together. We had worked on it for days, but no one showed up. Our volunteers felt so defeated, they wanted to quit. And to be honest, so did I. But at that moment, I looked outside and saw some young boys tossing stones at a boarded-up apartment building across the street. They were like boys in so many cities across the country—boys without prospects, without guidance, without hope. And I turned to the volunteers, and I asked them, "Before you quit, I want you to answer one question. What will happen to those boys?" And the volunteers looked out that window, and they decided that night to keep going—to keep organizing, keep fighting for better schools, and better jobs, and better health care. And so did I. And slowly but surely, in the weeks and months to come, the community began to change.

—Senator Barack Obama,
remarks on Super Tuesday,
February 5, 2008, Chicago, IL

[8]

Reach Out to Diverse Constituencies

Finally, those lines in my speech describe the demographic realities of America's future. Already, Texas, California, New Mexico, Hawaii, and the District of Columbia are majority minority. Twelve other states have populations that are more than a third Latino, black, and/or Asian. Latino Americans now number 42 million and are the fastest-growing demographic group, accounting for almost half of the nation's population growth between 2004 and 2005; the Asian American population, though far smaller, has experienced a similar surge and is expected to increase by more than 200 percent over the next 45 years. Shortly after 2050, experts project, America will no longer be a majority white country—with consequences for our economics, our politics, and our culture that we cannot fully anticipate.

—*Senator Barack Obama, "Race,"* The Audacity of Hope

THE CHALLENGE

There's an ethical and political imperative in embracing diversity, as America inevitably becomes more and more of a multiracial country. The statistics about growing minority populations are no secret, and they speak for themselves.

But there's another side to it. It's great to appreciate diversity and see it around you. We were struck with Obama's own appreciation of this when he worked as a community organizer in Chicago. He described it in *The Audacity of Hope:*

> As a young organizer, I often worked with Latino leaders on issues that affected both black and brown residents, from failing schools to illegal dumping to unimmunized children. My interest went beyond politics; I would come to love the Mexican and Puerto Rican sections of the city—the sounds of salsa and merengue pulsing out of apartments on hot summer nights, the solemnity of Mass in churches once filled with Poles and Italians and Irish, the frantic, happy chatter of soccer matches in the park, the cool humor of the man behind the counter at the sandwich shop, the elderly woman who would grasp my hand and laugh at my pathetic efforts at Spanish. I made lifelong friends and allies in those neighborhoods; in my mind, at least, the fates of black and brown were to be perpetually intertwined, the cornerstone of a coalition that could help America live up to its promise.

Obama sums up our point pretty well, no?

PRACTICAL INFORMATION

- In 2004, George W. Bush won four states, by margins of five percentage points or fewer, in which Hispanics make up a double-digit percentage of the electorate (New Mexico—37 percent, Florida—14 percent, Nevada—12 percent, and Colorado—12 percent). Obama won all these states in 2008.

- Only 23 percent of Hispanic voters align with the Republicans, while 57 percent lean toward the Democratic Party or call themselves Democrats. That's a 34 percent difference in partisan identification.

- The single-race white population is projected to remain almost flat from now until 2050, growing from 200 million to only 203 million.

- In 2050, 62 percent of American children are projected to be minorities (up from 44 percent today), and 38 percent are estimated to be single-race white (down from 56 percent today), pointing to the multiracial culture of the future.

(Source: Federal Election Commission, U.S. Census Bureau)

WHAT *YOU* CAN DO

Assist with naturalization workshops. As immigrants prepare to take their citizenship tests, they often need help learning civics and the basic history of America. In some communities, you can sign up to help. Nonprofit organizations that serve immigrant populations may offer "naturalization workshops" that help immigrants navigate the citizenship process.

Include Spanish-language media. If appropriate in your area, make sure your communications efforts include outreach to Spanish-language reporters. Don't be shy about sending English news releases to Spanish-language outlets.

Learn Spanish. This may be the challenge you've been looking for. You'll be surprised at all the enjoyment you'll have, especially if you can work it into your life—and vacations.

Produce literature in Spanish. Whenever it makes even the remotest sense, have your organizational or political literature translated into Spanish. This could even be justified if you live far away from Spanish-speaking populations, if you're creating a Web site addressing national issues. It's true that translations add a layer of complexity to any organizing task, but try to keep the big picture and the future of the country in mind.

Reach out. Make a point to include diversity in your own life. Invite different types of people to your home. Make friends with all types of people at work.

Volunteer. Don't be shy about volunteering. Ideally, you'll find a group in your area with which you have some sort of connection, but if not, pick up the phone and call.

RECOMMENDED RESOURCES

Center for Community Change, www.communitychange.org, is a champion of low-income people and communities of color.

Center for Social Inclusion, www.centerforsocialinclusion.org, develops and builds public will to make structural changes to address racial and class inequity.

Democracia U.S.A., www.democraciausa.org, promotes Hispanic civic engagement with multiple programs and state offices. The Web site is in English and Spanish.

Everyday Democracy, www.everyday-democracy.org/en/issue.6.aspx, helps communities develop their own ability to solve problems by exploring ways for all kinds of people to think, talk, and work together to create change.

Leadership Conference on Civil Rights, www.civilrights.org, is a resource for current news, events, reports, and diverse organizations.

The National Council of La Raza, www.nclr.org, is a Hispanic civil rights and advocacy group, with hundreds of affiliated organizations around the country. Click on "NCLR Affiliates" on its Web site to see if there's one in your area.

Pushback Network, www.pushbacknetwork.org, is a state-based group that emphasizes strategies to empower underrepresented constituencies: people of color, poor and working-class communities, and young people.

[9]

Attend a Leadership Training

And so, Take Back America, this is our time. Our time to make our mark on history, our time to write a new chapter in the American story, our time to lead a nation that is more prosperous and more free and more just than the one that we grew up in, so that someday, when our kids look back, they can say that this time of the dawn of the 21st century was when America renewed its purpose. They can say that this was a time when America found its way. They can say that this is a time when America learned to dream again. That's what this conference is about; that's what all of you are about.

—*Senator Barack Obama, "Take Back America" Conference,
June 14, 2006, Washington DC*

THE CHALLENGE

You might remember when vice-presidential candidate Sarah Palin told the Republican National Convention: "I guess a small-town mayor is sort of like a community organizer, except you have actual responsibilities."

It was ironic that Palin dismissed community organizers just as President Barack Obama's skilled and inspired community organizers were about to do a five-star job of sending Governor Palin back to Alaska.

Talk about actual responsibilities! Toppling McCain/Palin's campaign was a responsibility of the highest order, and Obama's people took it seriously, even though it wasn't simple. If you've ever tried to organize any community event, you know that even the easiest of organizing tasks is complex, and requires experience and training in multiple disciplines—not to mention the intangible quality of leadership.

Community organizers have historically picked up their professional training on the job, but today there are more opportunities to acquire organizing and leadership skills in a formal setting, from veterans, allowing you to learn in days what might have taken you months of wheel reinvention. And if you don't have the time for multi-day training, there's the option of learning from fellow activists over a weekend.

As President Obama said, "It's not that ordinary people have forgotten how to dream. It's just that their leaders have forgotten how." So the solution is to train ordinary people to be leaders.

PRACTICAL INFORMATION

- You can enroll in a training session as an individual, or members of your coalition can be trained together. Or you can find workshops on specific skills, like campaign work or online organizing.

- Training organizations frequently offer full or partial scholarships to those who apply and are accepted. Shop for different scholarship offerings.

- If you're working in a dysfunctional coalition—and there are a few out there in the grassroots organizing world—here's a course description from Rockwood Leadership that may inspire you to take leadership training, either at Rockwood or elsewhere: "The Art of Collective Leadership: A five-day intensive for networks and coalitions seeking greater collaborative skills and stronger vision and focus."

WHAT *YOU* CAN DO

Attend the "America's Future Now!" conference. The nation's largest conference of progressives takes place in early June. Speaking to the conference in 2006, Obama said, "And to all of you activists from all across the country, it's going to be because of you that we take our country back."

Donate to a leadership training organization. President Obama's election brought a new generation of community organizers into the political process. Now is a great time to train them. Give to one of the organizations listed at the end of this chapter.

Enroll in a training program for yourself or your organizing team. The number of national organizations offering high-quality training is growing steadily, as you can see from the partial list we've assembled in the recommended resources list below. If you decide to apply, ask your peers who work on similar issues or in your area if they know what's worked for them.

Have a drink and polish your organizing skills. Learn from your colleagues at a bar. Drinking Liberally has chapters around the country. Its motto: "Promoting democracy one pint at a time."

Organize your own leadership workshop. If a progressive training institute doesn't work for you, you might consider arranging your own training. You could ask an organizer in your community to work with you or your group on a limited basis. Or you can hire a progressive consultant (e.g., a campaign or communications consultant) to train you or your organization.

Participate in a Roots Camp. Look for conferences in your community that are organized from the bottom up, rather than the top down. Attendees can sign up to give a workshop—or attend one offered by others.

Start a political group around any social activity. A book club. Bowling. Gardening. Your group can have fun and be active politically at the same time. You might not take any political actions for a few meetings—and then dedicate an entire meeting to an action of some kind.

FROM THE FRONT LINES

We started this [America's Future Now! (formerly Take Back America)] when conservatives controlled everything and were leading the country off the cliff, and so we said there's gotta be a place where progressives gather across the tribes of progressive union members and MoveOn members and the hip-hop generation and civil rights activists and feminists to put a stake in the ground to say this is what we believe in and we're going to turn this country around.

—Robert Borosage, co-director of
Campaign for America's Future, which sponsors
the America's Future Now! conference

RECOMMENDED RESOURCES

Campaign for America's Future, www.ourfuture.org, runs the annual America's Future Now! conference (formerly "Take Back America") in Washington DC.

Center for Progressive Leadership, www.progressleaders.org, runs an array of community-organizing workshops.

New Organizing Institute, http://neworganizing.com, runs a progressive advocacy and campaign training program that focuses on online organizing.

Organizing for America, www.my.barackobama.com, helps people find local groups that have formed around a social activity. Or you can start one of your own by clicking on "My Groups" and inviting others to join. You'll be amazed at the breadth of topics already covered.

Young People For (YP4), www.youngpeoplefor.org, is a strategic, long-term leadership initiative launched by the People for the American Way Foundation to invest in the next generation of leaders and build a long-term national network for young progressives.

Progressive Majority, www.progressivemajority.org/training, is an organization that focuses on candidate training and development.

ProgressNow, www.progressnow.org, is a progressive online advocacy organization that provides an open-space format, known as rootscamp, where anyone can offer a topic to discuss.

Rockwood Leadership Program, www.rockwoodleadership.org, offers affordable leadership training for a wide range of social-change professionals.

Wellstone Action!, www.wellstone.org, is a national center for training and developing progressive leaders by continuing the work of Paul and Sheila Wellstone through training, educating, mobilizing, and organizing a vast network of progressive individuals and organizations.

10

Build a Neighborhood Team

But it was away from all that, as we prepared for our meeting with the Chicago Housing Authority director, that I began to see something wonderful happening. The parents began talking about ideas for future campaigns. New parents got involved. The block-by-block canvass we'd planned earlier was put into effect, with Linda and her swollen belly waddling door-to-door to collect complaint forms; Mr. Lucas, unable to read the forms himself, explaining to neighbors how to fill them out properly. Even those who'd opposed our efforts began to come around. . . . It was as though Sadie's small, honest step had broken into a reservoir of hope, allowing people in Altgeld [government housing] to reclaim a power they had had all along.

—*Community Organizer Barack Obama,*
"Chicago," Dreams from My Father

THE CHALLENGE

Barack Obama's presidential campaign used innovative web-based technology. The campaign built a massive organization of volunteers who visited the web to contact voters on behalf of the campaign.

But Obama's use of new technology, as impressive as it was, was only half the story.

The rest of the story is that Obama's campaign forged a new kind of organizing by combining the use of new technologies and online organizing with tried and true community-organizing methods. The Internet is an effective means of sharing information and making connections, but key Obama strategist and community-organizing guru Marshall Ganz recognized that people are mobilized, ultimately, through interpersonal relationships and a clear sense of shared values.

Ganz worked within the Obama campaign to revive community organizing through a program called "neighborhood teams." These neighborhood teams were encouraged to build relationships by sharing their personal stories. The teams were also encouraged to divide responsibilities and choose individual roles so that each team member had a clear sense of purpose and direction within the team.

Thousands of these neighborhood teams were built in communities across the country, creating what many believe was the largest field campaign in our nation's history. Many of these neighborhood teams have continued working together after the campaign to push for the policy changes that Obama promised in the election. New neighborhood teams also are beginning to form across the country, not just to elect candidates, but also to push for changes in policy at the local and state level and to work together on community service projects.

PRACTICAL INFORMATION

- The Obama campaign had millions of members on its Web site, tens of thousands of whom joined neighborhood teams across the country.

- There are more than 200 million people on Facebook and over 100 million on MySpace.

WHAT *YOU* CAN DO

Share your story with someone. Organizations are built on relationships. To organize your team, start by sharing your personal story with others in your area. What values motivate you? What in your life has moved you to work to create change?

Look for like-minded people on social networking sites. Millions of people are active on sites like Facebook or my.barackobama .com. Connect with these people online and invite them to join your team.

Start by figuring out who will be the team leaders. You can be one of them, plus a handful of others. Having a group of leaders shares the burden. And having roles gives each of you a clear sense of purpose within the team.

Hold a house party to bond and select issues to work on. Get to know each other and build relationships first, then talk about what you want to do.

Build your team around shared values, not particular issues. Particular issues come and go and some of them motivate us more than others. But the things that bind us over time are the values we share. Don't let those get lost as you work on different things.

Make a plan, with events relating to lobbying, education, and service. Team members might decide they care about environmental issues. For a community service event, they might raise money to buy seniors compact florescent light bulbs. For an education event, they might organize a lecture by an environmental author. And for a lobbying event, they might organize a rally in support of a bill in the state legislature. Invite community leaders and publicize all events—and sign up new folks.

Read the book *Rules for Radicals*. This is a timeless handbook about organizing by Saul D. Alinsky, founder of modern community organizing in America.

Set goals. There's nothing more empowering than getting stuff done. Set goals for events related to community service, grassroots lobbying, and education. Set a schedule of maybe one event per month.

Try to get training. You can reach out to national organizations for training for your team leaders, or possibly for everyone involved. See the chapter "Attend a Leadership Training."

Talk about what you're doing and why. A community service project might attract people who don't like politics. And the event itself, like a tree planting, can be a gentle way to begin discussing and learning about environmental issues and politics.

RECOMMENDED RESOURCES

Midwest Academy, www.midwestacademy.com, is a leading national training institute for the progressive movement based in Chicago.

New Organizing Institute, www.neworganizing.com, runs progressive advocacy campaigns and trainings.

Organizing for America, www.my.barackobama.com, helps people find local groups that have formed around a social activity. Or you can start one of your own by clicking on "My Groups" and inviting others to join.

ProgressNow, www.progressnow.org, is a national network of statewide groups primarily using online and neighborhood organizing tactics.

11

Call, Write, E-mail, or Meet Lawmakers

Thousands of you signed pledges of support, knocked on doors, made phone calls, and talked to your friends and neighbors about this budget and the investments it makes in our long-term prosperity. You showed Washington that ordinary citizens are demanding change and are willing to work for it.

—President Barack Obama,
The White House,
April 6, 2009, Washington DC

THE CHALLENGE

If all the people who complain that politicians are out of touch would actually try to stay in touch with their elected leaders, we guarantee politicians would be much more clued in to the stuff that matters.

You don't have to have an elaborate script to talk to them. All you need to do is know some basic facts and pick up the phone. It's more important that lawmakers see that you made the effort to contact them than it is that you have all your facts at the ready. We're not saying that you shouldn't write a decent letter or prepare for a phone call, but registering your opinion is what's most important.

Even the most cynical pundit would agree that contacting your lawmakers makes a difference—if enough of us do it.

PRACTICAL INFORMATION

- Only about one in five Americans contacts an elected official each year. This means that your voice may have a greater impact than you think.

- Some people are surprised at how easy it is to reach local lawmakers. Local elected officials, like school board members, probably have no staff at all. So don't assume a local politician has staffers screening you from them.

- It may take days or even weeks for a letter mailed via the postal service to arrive in congressional offices due to screening procedures. So take this into account when you decide how you want to contact lawmakers in Washington.

(Source: Pew Research Center for People and the Press)

WHAT *YOU* CAN DO

For phone calls...

Just do it. Many of us get an e-mail urging us to call a politician, and we think to ourselves, "Maybe I'll do it later." It takes only a few minutes to call, if you pick up the phone and get it done.

Ask for your lawmaker. If he or she isn't available, ask for the staffer who handles the issue that you are talking about. Treat the staff person as you would the lawmaker.

Don't spend too much time preparing. Know the basics. Most of the time, especially if you're calling your congressional representatives, you'll leave a message with the lowest staffer in the office—who keeps a tally of calls. So, really, all you need to know is the name of the bill you're concerned about and your position on it.

For e-mails and letters...

An e-mail is a weak way to communicate to Congress, because so many are sent there, but e-mails are fine for local officials. And they're better than nothing for Congress, too. If you don't hear anything after sending an e-mail, send it again.

Compose original, handwritten letters or e-mails. Form letters and postcards don't carry the weight of the old-fashioned letter.

Write in your own voice. Don't worry about being formal. Speak in your own words, and be as personal as possible. Funny or heartfelt letters have the most chance of getting passed up the chain of command in the office.

For meetings...

It's not always possible for an official to meet with you personally, and in fact, a meeting with a staffer can be more effective. Even if you're told in advance that you'll be meeting in person with your elected leader, you may find the staffer, not the official, in your meeting. That's OK. Treat staffers as you would the congressperson, as they may even be more critical to achieving your goal.

Assemble a group of about five people. Try to find folks who might not be expected to be on your side. Well-known community members are also influential.

Request your meeting by phone. Be ready to list who will attend the meeting and why you have an important perspective on the topic. You may be asked to put your request in writing.

Bring handouts. Don't cover more than one topic. Give your representative a packet (not exceeding five pages) of simple fact sheets and information about it. Endorsements (a newspaper editorial in favor of your legislation or letter from a honcho) or a list of endorsers are useful. Include a one-page summary of your position, with citations.

Practice in advance. No need to go crazy practicing, but we like to meet before a meeting to make sure everyone is clear on how the presentation will be delivered. Who will introduce the group? Who will make which points? To save time, your group can meet immediately prior to your scheduled meeting with your lawmaker, for a half hour or so.

Ask for precise answers. You can gently tell lawmakers that they're not answering a question, like you might tell anyone during the course of a conversation. Press them, without overdoing it.

Thank them, verbally and with a thank-you note that reinforces your main points.

RECOMMENDED RESOURCES

American Civil Liberties Union, http://action.aclu.org, provides information on how to meet with your elected officials in your district, not DC. Under "Action Network" on the sidebar find "Activist Toolkit." Click on that to reach the "ACLU Action Checklist." Scroll down to "Things You Can Do in Your Community." Under that is "Meet with Your Elected Representatives."

Congress.org, www.congress.org, provides way to find out who your elected officials are, as well as a comprehensive set of tips and tools for contacting your lawmakers. Look under "Issues and Actions."

20/20 Vision, www.2020vision.org/enhanceVoice.cfm#meeting, gives tips on all types of contact with legislators.

[12]

Throw a House Party for Change

I was skeptical at first, but unwilling as I was to discourage any initiative, I helped Will and Mary prepare a flyer for distribution along the block closest to the church. A week later, the three of us stood out on the corner in the late autumn wind. The street remained empty at first, the shades drawn down the rows of brick bungalows. Then, slowly, people began to emerge, one or two at a time, women in hairnets, men in flannel shirts or windbreakers, shuffling through the brittle gold leaves, edging toward the growing circle. When the gathering numbered twenty or so, Will explained that St. Catherine's was part of a larger organizing effort and that "we want you to talk to your neighbors about all the things y'all complain about when you're sitting at the kitchen table."

—*Community Organizer Barack Obama,*
"Chicago," Dreams from My Father

THE CHALLENGE

"I was inspired by Obama himself," says Shelley Flanagan. "I kept thinking, what more can I do?"

She'd knocked on doors, made calls, and donated. The idea to have a house party to raise money for Obama came when she was talking to a friend, David. He's a closet chef and his partner is a symphony-caliber pianist. They throw dinner parties where one cooks and the other plays the piano. For the Obama party, they prepared Latin American cuisine and played music from the same region, and Flanagan invited people and offered up her home. So in one room, you ate empanadas and flan. In the other, you heard Latin music on the piano.

"It felt so good, just coming together like that, and bringing people's talents together," Flanagan said. "David and Sam are shy, and this was something they could do. And I'm good at bringing people together."

In the end, Flanagan had to turn people away, after she had 70 RSVPs. She used the handy online tool on the Obama Web site to invite guests, not realizing that her invitation would be posted publicly. Before she knew it, she had 10 strangers sign up, but she'd already filled her party with friends. "So I had to backtrack on that," she said.

It makes sense that people wanted to come to her party, she says. "People who like Obama also like music and food."

PRACTICAL INFORMATION

- President Obama is using house parties now to mobilize support for his legislative agenda, among other things. For example, in February 2009, President Obama's grassroots organization, Organizing for America, listed over 3,000 house parties across country in support of the economic stimulus package.

- Political house parties are often aimed at raising money for a candidate, nonprofit group, or other cause. They also focus on registering voters, mailing in ballots, networking, or the like. Sometimes a house party may be the starting point for some other political activity, like going door to door.

- We like political house parties that try to be fun as well as purposeful. A themed event, like a potluck dinner with dishes featuring a type of food (like squash, for "squash Rush Limbaugh") or an ethnic cuisine, is a simple way to pull this off. You can easily connect a party to a holiday or date, like a big speech by Obama, Independence Day, the solstice, Presidents' Day—or how about a house party on Obama's birthday (August 4)?

WHAT *YOU* CAN DO

Get on the e-mail lists of Organizing for America and MoveOn. They'll suggest dates when house parties are being coordinated across the country.

Suggest a donation or action. With a group of people in the room, you should recommend actions at your house party. We think you should also ask for a "suggested donation," but some house-party hosts aren't comfortable with this. Another option is to state on your invitation that guests should bring their checkbooks.

E-invites are easy. Inviting people online via Organizing for America's Web site is really simple, even if you've never done it before. Or you can set up a Facebook group for your party. But a paper invitation or the phone works fine.

Tell your guests to invite their friends. Make sure you request an RSVP so you don't get too many people.

If your house or apartment won't work, try a picnic. Who needs a house for a house party?

Cut costs by having a potluck. Or at least request that others bring drinks.

Collect names. Collect contact information from your guests, and ask them to list friends who might help.

Sign up for Organizing for America, the president's outreach organization. It will let you know when grassroots actions, like house parties or meetings, are being coordinated to promote Obama's agenda.

Consider combining two goals at a single house party, for example, by raising money and educating people about Obama's legislation. Some parties feature a speech about an issue or candidate; others might center around a DVD or online video. Organizing for America sometimes provides such videos.

RECOMMENDED RESOURCES

The Center for Progressive Leadership, www.progressleaders.org, offers an online activist training workshop for use at a house party.

Democracy for America, www.democracyforamerica.com, provides campaign training, organizing resources, and media exposure for progressive issues and candidates.

Livingliberally.org, www.livingliberally.org, along with its counterpart, Drinking Liberally, promotes progressive action through social interaction and is a good resource to connect with folks in your area.

MoveOn, www.moveon.org, suggests house party ideas and has a huge national network of activists.

Organizing for America, www.barackobama.com, is a political group run by the Democratic National Committee founded just after President

Obama's inauguration. The group seeks to mobilize Obama supporters to elect other political candidates and support the president's legislative agenda. You can invite the public to your party via the President's Web site. You'll get house party ideas here, too. Click on "Organize Locally Using our Online Tools," and then "host an event." Follow the simple instructions, and you're on your way.

[13]

Testify at a Public
Hearing or Meeting

Sadie handed the microphone to Linda, who turned to the director and pointed to the stack of complaint forms. "Mr. Director. All of us in Altgeld [government housing] don't expect miracles. But we do expect basic services. That's all, just the basics. Now these people here have gone out of their way to fill out, real neat-like, all the things they keep asking the Chicago Housing Authority to fix but don't never get fixed. So our question is, will you agree here tonight, in front of all these residents, to work with us to make these repairs?"

—*Community Organizer Barack Obama,*
"Chicago," Dreams from My Father

THE CHALLENGE

As President Obama's community organizing experience shows, strategic use of public hearings can help communities win changes that improve their quality of life.

Many local governments—city councils, county commissioners, and the like—are required to hold their meetings in public. Often these meetings include a public comment period.

This chapter was contributed by Steve Kest, the executive director of the Association of Community Organizations for Reform Now (ACORN).

In addition, local governments and often boards and commissions—public utility commissions, environmental oversight committees, library boards, and others—hold hearings, often with invited "witnesses," on specific legislative proposals or broader issues over which they have jurisdiction.

These public meetings serve two purposes. The first is seeking public input into the decision-making process. Though we live in a world where the backroom deal is still alive and well, these venues provide an avenue for the average citizen to tell public and elected officials what they think of the proposals. The public comment period at a city council meeting is an example of this.

Public meetings are also an important leverage point for citizens to counteract the power and influence of lobbyists and their well-heeled clients. Usually, public meetings and hearings are dominated by corporations that have the time and money to understand complicated proposals and have a self-interested agenda to push.

But when average citizens show up in numbers, the playing field is more level, and the people can have their say. Not only are lobbyists and their clients blocked from dominating the proceedings, citizens that plan ahead can fill a hearing room with supporters all wearing the same T-shirts, hats, or buttons as a show of strength that carries as much weight as what is said at the podium.

PRACTICAL INFORMATION

- Many meetings and hearings are held at inconvenient times for people with jobs—often during the day. Public officials may reschedule meetings if you demand that they do so to accommodate working people. Of course, this may be impossible, but it could be worth a try if you've got a lot of people who will definitely show up if the time is changed.

- Many government entities have to publish a calendar of their public meetings and hearings. Visit the Web site of the entity in question, get on its e-mail list, or call the office to request calendar updates.

- Only about 20 percent of Americans say they take part in some form of "community problem solving" during the course of a year.

WHAT *YOU* CAN DO

Make sure you complete the paperwork. Most speaking opportunities require that people who wish to speak fill out "comment cards" (or the like) before the meeting starts. Don't lose your opportunity by failing to do the paperwork. This also means you need to arrive in time to do so—and be prepared to stay late.

Get your organization or group invited to give testimony at a hearing. A key way to build legitimacy in the eyes of decision-makers is to be invited to give testimony in front of the government body or commission. This doesn't happen by chance or out of the goodness of someone's heart. It happens because you make it happen. As part of your overall strategy to win on your issue, you should be building relationships with decision-makers that can result in an invitation to testify—either because they respect your leadership on the issue or because they can't afford to alienate you. Simply ask them to invite you.

Attend in numbers. Rarely do good ideas carry the day by themselves. One way to demonstrate the support for your idea or positions in the community is to make sure that the community is visible in its support. If you can, you should bring dozens of people with you. Or, as the old organizing adage says, "Don't bring plenty, bring twenty."

Prepare your presentation in advance. Most public comment periods in public hearings have limits on the amount of time anyone may speak, usually five minute or less. It is imperative that your presentation be concise and precise and that it fit the length of time.

Rehearse what you are going to say. It can be challenging speaking in public and you will help yourself by being familiar with what you are going to say, making it sound more like a conversation, and knowing that you are within the time limit.

Be prepared to spend a long time at the meeting or hearing. Public comment periods are often placed at the end of the agenda, and meetings can drag on for a long time. Bring a book or magazines to keep yourself occupied while you wait.

Whenever possible, make sure your presentation puts a "human face" on the problem. Statistics and numbers tell one part of the story, but telling the story of a person or family struggling with the issue at hand makes those numbers come to life, personalizing the problem for everyone to understand.

If you are part of a group working on an issue, try hard to ensure that your group is asked to provide testimony at the public hearing in question. This serves to convey legitimacy to your position and to your group, as well as giving you a larger platform to make your case directly to the decision-makers and to the public at large through any media coverage of the hearing.

RECOMMENDED RESOURCES

Citizens Write Plan C, www.citizenswriteplanc.com/testify.aspx, is a group of concerned citizens who formed in response to the two plans proposed by the Washington State Department of Transportation in regards to local ferry service. Their experience provides a sort of primer for testifying at public hearings.

The Epilepsy Foundation, www.epilepsyfoundation.org, offers advice on giving effective legislative testimony. Go to their Web site and type "legislative" in the search box.

LLRX.com, www.llrx.com/columns/guide35.htm, dedicated to providing research and technology to legal professionals, offers suggestions on how to testify before a public agency.

Oregon League of Conservation Voters Education Fund, www.olcveducation fund.org, has on its Web site a "citizen tool kit" for how to testify at a public hearing.

[14]

Get a Job to Help Change America

I was a young man then, just a year out of college; I knew no one in Chicago, was without money or family connections. But a group of churches had offered me a job as a community organizer for $13,000 a year. And I accepted the job, sight unseen, motivated then by a single, simple, powerful idea—that I might play a small part in building a better America.

—Senator Barack Obama,
in his declaration of candidacy,
February 10, 2007, Springfield, IL

THE CHALLENGE

Most great activists don't get paid for their work. They squeeze it in after their "real job." These are the kinds of people who have copy machines in their living rooms, flyers on their bookshelves, giant puppets of Ronald Reagan rotting in their backyards, and "pants-on-fire" Bush dolls piled in the basement next to the McCain's-head-is-in-the-sand-on-the-economy ostrich costume.

Paid activists have this kind of stuff in their offices—not necessarily their living rooms. Volunteer organizers do many of the same things as the paid ones do. Both are essential. But paid activists have more time to change the world, and if you're talented and motivated, we need you.

Maybe you're like President Obama was when he started out. You want to be a community organizer, but you don't know anyone who does it for a living.

There are many ways to do it. People work not just as organizers, but accountants, computer programmers, fundraisers, managers, writers, designers, producers, everything, or—at many small organizations— some combination of everything. You'd have to be incredibly small-minded to define a set of jobs that "help change America."

If you feel that your skills could be put to better use than they are now, consider the resources at the end of the chapter to help you get started.

You may find yourself in the same position as President Obama at the start of his career, when his vague notion to become a community organizer was realized.

PRACTICAL INFORMATION

- The nonprofit sector may contain the most jobs that focus on social change, but there are also lots of jobs in government as well as the private sector.

- America's nonprofit sector employs over 39 million people. Close to 5 million people volunteer in the sector full-time.

- The economic crisis has wounded nonprofit groups, as wealthy donors have cut back. At the same time, service-oriented organizations (like food banks and housing providers) are seeing the need for their services soar.

(Sources: John Hopkins University, Democratic Leadership Council)

WHAT *YOU* CAN DO

Check job banks. It's easier than ever to find specific lists of nonprofit or socially responsible jobs. There's our list below, but don't stop there. Most cities have their own sites, perhaps associated with a nonprofit program at a university or with the local nonprofit association. You'll find national lists focusing on specific skills too, like the sites we've listed below emphasizing communications skills.

Check job banks repeatedly. This is basic job-hunting, but employers are often in a rush once they make a decision to hire. So jump on job offerings quickly.

Get an internship. Consider volunteering or applying for a formal internship at an organization that interests you. It's often the best way to get in the door. And if you don't end up getting hired there, you might make contacts with similar outfits in need of employees.

Network. Scour your friends and family for connections in the field that interests you. Get the names of those connections, call them, and ask to meet for coffee, even if they have no jobs themselves. Ask for names of others you can call in the field.

Make your current job better. If you can't find another job, check the Web site for Businesses for Social Responsibility, (www.bsr.org), which has suggestions for how any business can act more ethically.

RECOMMENDED RESOURCES

The Communications Network, www.comnetwork.org/resources/jobs.html, lists communications jobs at foundations, nonprofits, and elsewhere. (Also see www.truespinconference.com/jobs.)

Democratic Gain, www.democraticgain.org, is an organization with a "job and talent" bank, as well as other information to support the "professional needs of individuals and organizations that work in Democratic or progressive politics."

Green Careers Center, www.environmentalcareer.com, provides an excellent job board of environmental positions and green employers.

The Foundation Center, http://foundationcenter.org/getstarted/guides/job.html, lists jobs in the foundation and philanthropy world, broken down by state.

Idealist.org, www.idealist.org, posts thousands of socially responsible jobs in various categories, located in the United States and internationally. Also find volunteer opportunities, organizations, and more.

New Organizing Institute, www.neworganizing.com/resources/jobs, provides an electronic mailing list of new jobs, many in the new media sector.

NonProfit-jobs.org, www.nonprofit-jobs.org, is a job board for nonprofits and government positions across the country.

Progressive Exchange, www.progressiveexchange.org, lists jobs with a focus on online advocacy and organizing.

[15]

Support Political Art

We have to just improve arts and music funding generally—in schools but also outside of schools. And the endowment for the arts, our support of the public arts, our support for arts institutions—all those things should be a priority. And they don't cost that much money. They really don't. But you get such a big payoff. And one last point...part of what arts education does is it teaches people to see each other through each other's eyes. It teaches us to respect and understand people who are not like us. And that makes us better citizens and makes our democracy work better, and that's something I strongly believe in.

—Senator Barack Obama,
Town Hall Meeting,
April 2, 2008, Wallingford, PA

THE CHALLENGE

Meagen Svendsen had wanted to make a political statement for years, but as an artist, she hadn't really had the inclination. Barack Obama's candidacy inspired her to try.

When Democrats announced that the Democratic National Convention would be coming to Denver, Svendsen had the idea of organizing fellow artists to create artwork with a convention theme. So the art show, "Artists Against Convention," was born. It eventually attracted over 60 submissions of art for 30 spots, which were showcased at a local gallery. Svendsen wasn't against the Democratic Convention, but she chose an edgy name for her show to generate media interest.

"The show highlighted Denver's wide range of artistic talent, offered alternative views on the political process in our country, and, hopefully, inspired some dialogue on the subject," Svendsen told us.

It succeeded. Svendsen's art show was covered by the local daily newspaper, the public radio station, an alternative weekly, and more.

Political art shows like Svendsen's get media attention not only because they offer a visual connection to political issues but also because artists often have controversial perspectives on the current political debate. For example, titles of pieces in Svendsen's show included "No More Cages," "Race," and "Under Surveillance."

It was a bit of a stretch for Svendsen to call news reporters and pitch her show, but she wanted to do something for the cause of remaking America.

PRACTICAL INFORMATION

- Artists are natural allies for activists seeking change, and their skills can add depth and impact to a community organizer's arsenal. They can help with sign painting, political theater, costume making, and much more. Many political activists consider themselves artists, and many artists see themselves as activists.

- The Internet offers political artists a huge avenue to have a greater impact. As Kristin Gorski wrote on the Huffington Post, "Paper posters plastered on walls throughout towns used to be the primary means of sharing political slogans; technology has amplified the town square, and the walls are now digital."

- Sometimes political activists and political artists who share broad goals will part ways over what's the right "message" and how it should be delivered. Community organizers are focused on how their political message will be received by their target audiences, whom they want to win over. Artists, on the other hand, are often unconcerned about offending people, even those who might agree with their point. They're frequently more interested in political expression for its own sake.

WHAT *YOU* CAN DO

Pitch your political art-show idea to a local gallery first, rather than renting a space and setting up the show yourself. A gallery sponsorship gives the show more credibility. If you can't find a gallery, a non-gallery space can work just fine. Or your art show can take place for a single day on the sidewalk or a closed street.

Find a pair of local celebrity types to judge the art. A talk show host, pundit, or a local politician, for example, would add news value to the show.

Pick a theme that's tied to an issue that you expect to be in the news when your show opens to the public. Svendsen's show was tied to the Democratic Convention. That was perfect, in part because the local media were scrambling around in the weeks prior to the convention looking for angles on it to cover. An artist's perspective offered journalists a new angle.

Distribute a press release offering the public a chance to create art for the show. Then put out another news release when the show is going to open.

Give journalists an opportunity to view the art show at a convenient time, like around noon a few days before it opens. Don't simply invite journalists to the show's opening on a Friday night. That's a bad time to get coverage.

Give your judges clear guidelines for judging the work.

RECOMMENDED RESOURCES

Americans for the Arts, www.artsusa.org, supports culture and the arts. Sign up for their advocacy alerts.

Art of Democracy, http://artofdemocracy.ning.com, provides networking opportunities for political artists.

Artists for Obama, http://my.barackobama.com/page/group/artistsfor obama, is one of many groups that formed during the president's election campaign. You can form a group, too, on www.my.barack obama.com.

Backbone Campaign, www.backbonecampaign.org, has classes and ready-made art that you can use—or borrow—for press events and other visibility efforts.

Bread and Puppet Theater, www.breadandpuppet.org, is an organization that makes beautiful puppets for protests and theater.

Meaningful Media, www.meaningfulmedia.org, is a nonprofit network committed to changing our world through media, including art forms. Sign up for their updates.

[16]

Open Doors for Young People

I've met countless people of all ages and walks of life who want nothing more than to do their part. I've seen a rising generation of young people work and volunteer and turn out in record numbers. They're a generation that came of age amidst the horrors of 9/11 and Katrina; the wars in Iraq and Afghanistan; an economic crisis without precedent. And yet despite all this, or more likely because of it, they have become a generation of activists possessed with that most American of ideas—that people who love their country can change it.

—*President Barack Obama signing the Edward M. Kennedy Serve America Act at the SEED School, April 21, 2009, Washington DC*

THE CHALLENGE

How do we keep President Obama's momentum alive? There are lots of partial answers to this question, which is central to our book. But the question is especially important for all the young people who President Obama has brought into the political process.

Young people took a starring role in Obama's election campaign. There was endless speculation about whether they'd turn out, burn out, space out, and whatever else, and in the end, they delivered—not only in terms of votes but in creating a campaign energy that was devastating to Obama's opponents and inspiring to the rest of us.

Now it's up to all of us, young people themselves and the not-so-young, to pay particular attention to giving young people opportunities to gain more experience in politics—and to allow them to create their own opportunities.

We've listed some specific suggestions, but in the broadest sense, now is a time to pay extra attention to young people who cross our lives, whether they're family or friends or job seekers. Obama has created an opportunity for them to understand politics and their communities in a different way than previous generations.

PRACTICAL INFORMATION

- President Obama took 66 percent of the vote among 18- to 29-year-olds, according to exit polls.

- Millennials, born between 1977 and 1998, are nearly 45 million strong. By 2015, the millennial generation will make up one-third of the electorate.

- Thirty-nine percent of Millennials identify as non-white, making them the most diverse generation in American history. Young Latinos account for the largest percentage of the population boom.

(Source: Young Democrats of America)

WHAT *YOU* CAN DO

Donate money to political organizations serving young people. Some are listed in the recommended resources section, but there are many others.

Pay for a young person to attend an organizing workshop or progressive conference. These opportunities can change a person's life. See options in our chapter, "Attend a Leadership Training."

Register a young person to vote. Find young people in your world who are not registered to vote, and make sure they register. Then make sure they vote.

Mentor a young person, informally. Make an extra effort to help out youths who share Obama's progressive values. Hook them up with people you know in your community. Stay in touch. Nurture the generational shift, if it's happening, toward progressive values.

RECOMMENDED RESOURCES

Bus Project, www.busproject.org, is a national model which has mobilized thousands of volunteers and activists around the state of Oregon and throughout the country.

League of Young Voters, www.theleague.com, focuses on engaging young people in politics, especially from communities of color and low-income communities.

Rock the Vote, www.rockthevote.org, uses music and pop culture to encourage voter registration and political action among young people.

Young Democrats of America, www.yda.org, has chapters across the country mobilizing youths to support Democrats.

Young People For, www.youngpeoplefor.org, launched by the People For the American Way Foundation, runs community-organizing workshops for young people.

[17]

Organize Your Place of Worship

In the end, then, what is called for is nothing more, and nothing less, than what all the world's great religions demand—that we do unto others as we would have them do unto us. Let us be our brother's keeper, scripture tells us. Let us be our sister's keeper. Let us find that common stake we all have in one another, and let our politics reflect that spirit as well.

—Senator Barack Obama,
"A More Perfect Union" speech,
March 18, 2008, Philadelphia, PA

THE CHALLENGE

When Obama talks about connecting political and spiritual values, he speaks to most of America. About a third of U.S. citizens attend their place of worship weekly, over half say religion is important in their lives, and about 80 percent believe in heaven.

Religion can be a powerful force in American politics, as demonstrated by the civil rights movement of the 1960s or the more recent evangelical support of President George W. Bush. But as a bumper sticker we saw puts it, "God isn't a Republican or a Democrat." So if you're connected to a church, temple, mosque, or other place of worship, you may have access to a group of people who will hear Obama's words about the importance of faith to politics—and who will be inspired to take concrete actions to join our president in trying to make the world a better place.

As Obama said when he was a community organizer:

> Over the past few years, however, more and more young and forward-thinking pastors have begun to look at community organizations . . . as a powerful tool for living the social gospel, one which can educate and empower entire congregations and not just serve as a platform for a few prophetic leaders. Should a mere 50 prominent black churches, out of the thousands that exists in cities like Chicago, decide to collaborate with a trained organizing staff, enormous positive changes could be wrought in the education, housing, employment, and spirit of inner-city black communities, changes that would send powerful ripples throughout the city.
>
> (*From "Why Organize? Problems and Promise in the Inner City," first published in the August/September 1988 issue of university publication* Illinois Issues)

PRACTICAL INFORMATION

- The tax status of most religious institutions prohibits them from endorsing candidates, but nonpartisan political activities (like voter registration, political debate, or feeding the poor) are allowed.

- The more frequently Americans attend worship services, the more likely they are to hold conservative political opinions. For example, about 60 percent of citizens who go to religious services once a week or more say that abortion should be made mostly or completely illegal, while about 30 percent who attend less frequently espouse this political opinion.

- Seventy-eight percent of Americans identify as Christian and 16 percent as unaffiliated. About five percent align with other religions, including 1.7 percent with Judaism, 0.7 percent with Buddhism, and 0.6 percent with Islam.

(Source: The Pew Forum on Religion and Public Life)

WHAT *YOU* CAN DO

Start a voter registration drive. Registering people to vote is widely accepted as appropriate for religious institutions. Voter registration drives are conducted by activists at their places of worship or at community events.

Become a partner with the Census. See our chapter, "Help the Census Count Everybody."

Lobby your congregation leader. Some congregation leaders reference current events in their services. Consider buying your congregation leader a subscription to the online service "Preaching the Word," a monthly compilation of tips on connecting social justice to the scriptures put out by the editors of *Sojourners,* who describe it as being for "those who preach 'with the Bible in one hand and the newspaper in the other.'" Also, if appropriate for your faith, give your congregation leader the names of people who might actually deliver the sermon, as guests.

Work with the social justice group. A social justice committee within a place of worship is often in charge of community service work, such as food drives or voter registration. Or it might distribute nonpartisan voter guides. Find out what it's up to and see if members want to undertake any actions from this book. If no justice committee exists in your place of worship, ask your congregational leader about starting one.

RECOMMENDED RESOURCES

Catholics in Alliance for the Common Good, www.catholicsinalliance.org, promotes awareness of the Catholic Social Tradition and its core values of justice, human dignity, and the common good to Catholics, the media, and Americans of all faiths.

Religious Action Center of Reform Judaism, www.rac.org, is a progressive Jewish organization concerned with social justice and legislative issues.

Sojourners, www.sojo.net, is a Christian ministry devoted to social justice and has lots of material for progressive Christians.

United Church of Christ, www.ucc.org, has guides on its Web site for how to organize the faith community. Click "Change the World."

Volunteer in Your Community

I urge you to get involved, right now, at this defining moment in history. I'm not going to tell you what your role should be; that's for you to discover. And I won't promise that it will always be easy or that you'll accomplish all your goals all at once. But as I learned in the shadow of an empty steel plant more than two decades ago, while you can't necessarily bend history to your will, you can do your part to see that it, in the words of Dr. King, "bends toward justice." So I hope that you will stand up and do what you can to serve your community, shape our history, and enrich both your own life and the lives of others across this country.

—President Barack Obama,
"A New Era of Service Across America,"
Time *magazine, March 19, 2009*

[18]

Respond to Obama's
Call for National Service

It's as simple as that. All that's required on your part is a willingness to
make a difference. That is, after all, the beauty of service. Anyone can
do it. You don't need to be a community organizer, or a Senator—or
a Kennedy—or even a President to bring change to people's lives.

—President Barack Obama, signing the Edward M. Kennedy
Serve America Act at the SEED School,
April 21, 2009, Washington DC

THE CHALLENGE

Take a break from reading this book for a few minutes and sign up to
receive regular information from President Obama's national service
initiative.

Find a volunteer opportunity online at www.serve.gov. Signing up
takes a minute, and then you might peruse the Web site for a while
before returning to this book. You'll find that you can search for volunteer opportunities near your home. Some of the categories of work
include blood drives, food banks, shelters, health, training, environment,
clean-up, and neighborhood. You can post your own event that involves
volunteers, or you can sign up for those posted by others.

"Find a Volunteer Opportunity" on the Web site lists other estab-
lished volunteer programs across the country. These are useful because,

as we're writing this chapter, Obama's volunteer program is just getting off the ground, and the options are more limited than we hope they'll be in the future.

PRACTICAL INFORMATION

- If you think you're watching TV too much, consider volunteering. People who volunteer in their communities spend eight hours less watching TV than non-volunteers (15 hours per week for volunteers versus 23 hours for non-volunteers).

- A volunteer project is a good way to keep your political group together. If you're not sure what to do now that President Obama is in office, you might consider a regular service activity for your group—until you switch back to political activities. See our chapter "Build a Neighborhood Team."

- The Edward M. Kennedy Serve America Act, already signed by President Obama, expands AmeriCorps, strengthens the nonprofit sector, expands opportunities for volunteerism, and establishes September 11 as our country's National Day of Service.

(Source: Time *magazine)*

FROM THE FRONT LINES

As President Obama has said—and knows from experience—working directly in our communities is a critical step towards making the change we all want. Change doesn't always come in the form of new policies and government programs. It can come from all of us putting our values into action each day in ways big and small. We don't have to wait for others to act; we can take care of community needs today.

—Thomas Bates, co-founder of Democrats Work

WHAT *YOU* CAN DO

Find volunteer events and jobs in the recommended resources section. We've listed Web sites that aggregate different types of volunteer opportunities, as well as specific organizations that need volunteers. And of course, there are many others in your community that aren't listed.

Volunteer in response to a crisis. After Hurricane Katrina, people from all over America went to Louisiana to help out. If a disaster hits our country—or another one—consider a trip to help out on the ground.

Tell the White House about your community service. Tell your story at www.whitehouse.gov/change.

RECOMMENDED RESOURCES

AmeriCorps, www.americorps.gov, is America's community service program, started by Bill Clinton. Their volunteers work in schools, parks, and more. The Edward M. Kennedy Serve America Act increases slots in AmeriCorps from 75,000 to 250,000 by 2017.

BoardNetUSA, www.boardnetusa.org, connects nonprofits looking for board members with those seeking to serve on a nonprofit board.

Citizen Schools, www.citizenschools.org, connects middle school students with volunteer "citizen teachers" who lead hands-on, after-school classes in dozens of states.

Corporation for National and Community Service, www.freedomcorps.gov, is a White House project whose Web site lists volunteer opportunities nationwide.

Democrats Work, www.democratswork.org, is an organization that mobilizes grassroots Democrats to perform community service projects . . . as Democrats.

Meals on Wheels Association of America, www.mowaa.org, works toward the social, physical, nutritional, and economic betterment of vulnerable Americans and provides programs to make a difference in the lives of others. Volunteer locally by going on their Web site and clicking on "Take Action."

National Park Service, www.nps.gov/gettinginvolved/index.htm, lists ways to help protect and preserve our National Parks.

Prison Dharma Network, www.prisondharmanetwork.org, seeks volunteers for a nonsectarian, contemplative support network for prisoners, prison volunteers, and corrections professionals.

USA Service, www.usaservice.org, is President Obama's Web site, which calls for citizens to engage in community service projects. You can find projects you're interested in, post your own, or organize with others to create a joint project.

VolunteerMatch, www.volunteermatch.org, provides a listing of specific volunteer opportunities in your area.

Volunteers of America, www.voa.org, posts human-service volunteer jobs all over the country. Click on the "Get Involved" link in the upper right hand corner of this Web site to find ones that interest you.

Youth Service America, www.ysa.org, focuses on volunteer opportunities for young people, aged 5 to 25.

[19]

Help the Homeless

At a time when there are children in the city of New Orleans who still spend each night in a lonely trailer, we need more of you to take a weekend or a week off from work, and head down South, and help rebuild. If you can't get the time, volunteer at the local homeless shelter or soup kitchen in your own community.

—*Senator Barack Obama,*
Wesleyan University Commencement,
May 25, 2008, Middletown, CT

THE CHALLENGE

Today, as we're writing this chapter, the *New York Times* is reporting that modern-day Hoovervilles have appeared in about a dozen U.S. cities. They obviously aren't as large or widespread as the Depression-era shantytowns, but they're a sign of the times.

A reporter asked President Obama about the shantytowns during a recent news conference, and he said that it was "not acceptable for children and families to be without a roof over their heads in a country as wealthy as ours."

Who wouldn't agree, even now, when economic times are tough? So here are a few ideas on how you can do your part to help.

PRACTICAL INFORMATION

- One in 10 U.S. households is at risk of going hungry or is experiencing hunger now. This includes 13 million children.

- Over 13 percent of the U.S. population lives in poverty, and about a third of these people are children.

(Sources: U.S. Department of Agriculture, U.S. Census, Labor Department)

WHAT *YOU* CAN DO

Donate money, food, or clothing to organizations serving the homeless. In Obama's Illinois headquarters, a sign was posted on the door to the bathroom asking staffers to bring hotel shampoo and soap to donate to homeless shelters.

Volunteer at a homeless shelter or food bank. Volunteers help with everything (cooking, cleaning, serving, and counseling) at these service organizations.

Teach your children about homelessness. Here's a federal government Web site for kids to learn about homelessness and what to do to help: www.hud.gov/kids/hthsplsh.html.

Give away food you grow. If you're inspired by the Obamas' White House garden and plant your own, you'll almost certainly get extra food in the fall. You no longer have to drop your extra zucchinis on your neighbor's porch and run away! Organize your fellow backyard gardeners and give your extra produce to those who need it. The Garden Writers Association's "Plant a Row for the Hungry" program will help you set up a program in your area—or connect with an existing one. Get details at www.gardenwriters.org or call 877-492-2727.

Organize a food or clothing drive at work. A simple idea that takes little time and is usually well received by everyone. (You can expand on this by recruiting other businesses to participate.)

Raise awareness about homelessness. Don't just ignore the problem. Ask your friends what they're doing to help. Ask your congregation leader to collect money or food for the homeless and discuss their situation at your place of worship.

RECOMMENDED RESOURCES

Association of Gospel Rescue Missions, www.agrm.org, runs a network of rescue missions. The Web site includes a directory.

Department of Housing and Urban Development, www.hud.gov/homeless/index.cfm, is the section of the federal agency's Web site on homelessness and how to help.

Feeding America, www.feedingamerica.org, is a directory of food banks and advice.

Habitat for Humanity, www.habitat.org/cd/local/default.aspx, builds houses for the homeless. Their Web site can show you how to volunteer in your area.

National Coalition for the Homeless, www.nationalhomeless.org, has lots of information about how to help, including a directory of local homeless service organizations.

[20]

Assist Your Local Library

Right now, children come home from their first doctor's appointment with an extra bottle of formula. But imagine if they came home with their first library card or their first copy of *Goodnight Moon?*

—*Senator Barack Obama,*
"Literacy and Education in a 21st-Century Economy,"
June 27, 2005, Boston, MA

THE CHALLENGE

By supporting your local library, you're doing a lot more than helping pay for books or computers or DVDs. You're standing up for literacy and the health of your community, because if you look at all the things libraries do, you realize that at their heart, they're advocates for literacy and a community of people who value it.

Public libraries support the ability and desire of people to understand each other and the world. That ability is the foundation of what's needed to make the change that President Obama articulates.

How many people remember from childhood reading books at the local library with other kids and the librarian? Or the volunteer who helped figure out what you were talking about?

When you combine the sense of community with the information that you get from a library, you understand why supporting them fits so well with Obama's vision for America.

PRACTICAL INFORMATION

- As it has in the past when the economy has sunk, library usage is surging during the economic crisis. Attendance and circulation are up by double digits in some areas.

- Asked how many books they read in the past year, the average American answered four, and one out of four of us read no books at all.

- Just over 9 percent of 16- to 24-year-olds in the United States are high-school dropouts, but the literacy rate in the United States is 99 percent.

(Sources: Boston Globe, *Associated Press, National Center for Educational Statistics)*

WHAT *YOU* CAN DO

Volunteer. Libraries will train volunteers to teach computer skills, answer questions, shelve books, serve homebound citizens, and more. Check your library's Web site for the specific needs of your local library.

Read aloud to kids in the local library. To us, story time at the library is one of the greatest ways to promote literacy at the grassroots level. Libraries often need volunteers to do it. Some libraries provide read-aloud programs for organizations like Head Start.

Go to library fund-raising events. Libraries have galas, used book sales, and awards. Public libraries may be linked to a foundation that needs board members, fund-raisers, or other help. You can also donate directly to your local library.

Donate stuff to the library. Books. DVDs. Computers. CDs. Magazine subscriptions. Find out what your local library needs. Libraries in local jails and prisons also are always in need of donated books and magazines.

Patronize the library gift shop. Libraries in larger cities have one.

Help the librarian at your local school. School librarians are feeling the pain of tight education budgets, and they need your help. Call your local school and talk to the librarian.

Participate in the Campaign for America's Libraries. Keep track of national events related to libraries. Visit the American Library Association's Web site for details.

RECOMMENDED RESOURCES

American Library Association, www.ala.org, keeps track of library-related federal legislation, promotions, and developments in the library world nationally.

Your Public Library. Check out the Web site of your local library. You'll probably find a link to information on how to volunteer and an explanation of what volunteers do. If not, call for information on volunteering—or for answers to any other questions about supporting libraries.

[21]

Support Our Troops and Veterans

We must also do our part, not only as a nation, but as individuals, for those Americans who are bearing the burden of wars being fought on our behalf. That can mean sending a letter or a care package to our troops overseas. It can mean volunteering at a clinic where a wounded warrior is being treated or bringing supplies to a homeless veterans center. Or it can mean something as simple as saying "thank you" to a veteran you pass on the street.

That is what Memorial Day is all about. It is about doing all we can to repay the debt we owe to those men and women who have answered our nation's call by fighting under its flag. It is about recognizing that we, as a people, did not get here by accident or good fortune alone...

It's about remembering each and every one of those moments when our survival as a nation came down not simply to the wisdom of our leaders or the resilience of our people, but to the courage and valor of our fighting men and women. For it is only by remembering these moments that we can truly appreciate a simple lesson of American life—that what makes all we are and all we aspire to be possible are the sacrifices of an unbroken line of Americans that stretches back to our nation's founding.

—President Barack Obama,
Memorial Day weekend address,
May 23, 2009, Washington DC.

THE CHALLENGE

During the election, on Veterans Day, we organized a press conference with a half dozen veterans. We wanted to spotlight the need for the next president to treat veterans better than the last one.

Not a single reporter showed up. This happens sometimes, as you know if you've organized press conferences. Sometimes competing news overwhelms yours. You just hope to do better next time.

But sitting there with the veterans, waiting for reporters to come, was sad. It felt too much like a metaphor for how our country treats its vets, who account for a heartbreaking 25 percent of all homeless people in America. It's not right.

And our active troops also deserve better treatment. To us, "support the troops" has meant, first and foremost, pulling them out of Iraq. Even though President Obama has announced that most will be coming home, the antiwar movement is still important. The Afghanistan situation is potentially disastrous for our troops and for Afghanistan, and Iraq is by no means solved for us or the Iraqis.

But there's a lot more to do for the troops and our veterans here at home. It's not just a matter of supporting them because it's patriotic. As President Obama says, we really are in debt to our veterans, for fighting for our country, whether the decision to deploy them was right or wrong. We are complicit in any decision to go to war, even if we didn't vote for the commander-in-chief who actually sent our troops overseas.

PRACTICAL INFORMATION

- About 150,000 American veterans are homeless on a given night.

- From 1997 to 2007, nearly 10,000 personnel were released from the military for violating the "don't ask, don't tell" policy.

- About 23 million U.S. citizens are veterans, including over 250,000 who are completely disabled.

- Over 4,250 U.S. troops have died in Iraq, and over 31,000 have been injured.

(Sources: National Coalition for Homeless Veterans, USA Today, Veterans Administration, icasualties.org)

WHAT *YOU* CAN DO

Support a veterans group. You can donate or volunteer for one of the groups listed below. Find others on the Web sites listed.

Help reverse the military's "don't ask, don't tell" policy. Under this discriminatory policy, openly gay individuals cannot serve in the military. Veterans can sign a petition on the Web site of Vote Vets (votevets.org), to reverse it. (President Obama has promised to reverse this policy, but has yet to do so.)

Organize an event showing the human cost of the Iraq War. The American Friends Service Committee has a free manual on how you can stage an "Eyes Wide Open" exhibit on campus or anywhere. Using boots to symbolize Iraqi casualties, the exhibit is fairly easy to set up with the help of AFSC's step-by-step guide available online.

Take Veterans Day seriously. You can do everything from attending events and donating to simply talking about veterans and war. Fly the flag—or buy one for someone who doesn't. It's usually observed on November 11.

RECOMMENDED RESOURCES

American Friends Service Committee, www.afsc.org, is a pacifist organization
with chapters across the country. You can receive a biweekly update
with information about peace issues and organizing resources.

National Coalition for Homeless Veterans, www.nchv.org/howtohelp.cfm,
is part of a national network that provides resources for veteran
support groups in your area. You can help in numerous ways.

National Priorities Project, www.nationalpriorities.org/costofwar_home, is
a research group that illuminates how much the federal government
spends on competing priorities, for example, the Iraq War versus
education in your state. Budget tradeoffs are also highlighted, such
as how many teachers could be hired for the costs of fighter jets.

Support Your Vet, www.supportyourvet.org, furnishes information on how
to help veterans from Iraq and Afghanistan. It is designed for vets'
families and friends, but others can find ways to help here too.

U.S. Department of Veterans Affairs, www1.va.gov/VSO/index.cfm?
template=view, lists veterans service organizations.

Vote Vets, www.votevets.org, is a veterans group that led the campaign
to pull troops from Iraq and is quick to respond to the needs of
troops.

[22]

Volunteer at a School

But we know that government alone is not the answer to the challenges we face. Yes, our government must rebuild our schools, but we also need people to serve as mentors and tutors in those schools.

—*President Barack Obama, "A New Era of Service across America,"* Time *magazine, March 19, 2009*

THE CHALLENGE

Even if you think you're following the plight of public education, you'll probably find you don't understand much about education until you volunteer in a public school. We volunteer at our kids' schools, and we can tell you that trying to teach a struggling kid how to do long division is one of the most gratifying and illuminating experiences you'll ever have.

There are lots of ways to volunteer. You can help teach kids yourself, by tutoring them or working with them, or you can contribute behind the scenes at a school. Either way, you'll be on the front lines of change in America.

You can volunteer at a school even if you don't have time to go there during the day. Teachers have lots of take-home work to do, including grading papers, cutting materials, doing research, and much more. By taking this stuff off a teacher's plate, you're freeing up more time to spend with students.

And you'll probably learn as much from the kids as they will from you.

PRACTICAL INFORMATION

- The average class size in America is about 25 students. There are about 3.2 million public school teachers in the United States.

- Most of the funding for public schools comes from state and local governments, not the feds. The federal government contributed about 9 percent of funding for public schools serving kindergarten through 12th grade.

- About 80 percent of prisoners do not have a high school diploma.

- Among U.S. children attending public schools, 60 percent cannot do math at grade level and 66 percent cannot read at grade level. Eighty-five percent of black children don't do grade-level math, versus half of white kids and 78 percent of Hispanic children.

- Research and common sense tell you that academic achievement and confidence are linked to parental involvement, at home and in school.

(Sources: National Education Association, Children's Defense Fund)

WHAT *YOU* CAN DO

Find a School. If you have a child or relative in school, you probably want to volunteer at that school. If not, then visit your school district's Web site and identify the government agency or nonprofit group that manages volunteers, for example, the San Francisco School Volunteers. If there isn't such an organization, pick a school and set up a meeting with the principal.

Volunteer where you're needed. It's fun to volunteer at your neighborhood school, but you may also decide to select a school that is in more need of help. To do this, look at the statistics about a school on your school district's Web site. Note the percentage of kids who receive a free or reduced-price lunch, as this is an indicator of poverty. Also check out standardized test scores. Lower-performing schools with kids in poverty need more help.

Ask how you can help. "Don't impose yourself on the school," said Lisa Spinali, executive director of San Francisco School Volunteers. "The first question is 'How can I help you?'"

Join school committees. The governing bodies of some schools have a dedicated slot for a community representative.

Tell educators about your skills. Perhaps you've got coaching or tutoring experience.

As a school volunteer, be solid and reliable, particularly for kids who lack consistency in other parts of their lives. You should take your volunteer commitment seriously, perhaps more than you might another volunteer task. This means you should stick with it for at least a semester and dedicate a set amount of time, such as an hour a week.

RECOMMENDED RESOURCES

Citizen Schools, www.citizenschools.org/volunteer, provides opportunities for folks to volunteer in schools in select cities.

Hands On Schools, www.behandson.org/hands-on-schools, explains how communities can develop successful relationships with schools. Check out its how-to manual, "Hands On School Box."

Project Appleseed, www.projectappleseed.org, is an educational resource and advocate for parents and families engaged in America's public schools.

San Francisco School Volunteers, www.sfsv.org, has been a national model for volunteers in local schools for over 45 years.

VolunteerMatch, www.volunteermatch.org, provides a listing of volunteer opportunities by area, including many in education.

[23]

Spread Change Worldwide

To the people of poor nations, we pledge to work alongside you to make your farms flourish and let clean waters flow; to nourish starved bodies and feed hungry minds. And to those nations like ours that enjoy relative plenty, we say we can no longer afford indifference to suffering outside our borders; nor can we consume the world's resources without regard to effect. For the world has changed, and we must change with it.

—President Barack Obama, inaugural speech,
January 20, 2009, Washington DC

THE CHALLENGE

The positive international reaction to President Obama's election was truly gratifying—and a relief. After seeing so much of the world react with such apparent surprise and approval at his victory, we were even more proud that we elected him.

President Obama's sensitivity to the struggles of developing countries creates an opening for us to show the world, substantively, why we deserve respect. And that we care. There is a lot that can be done by the federal government in addition to pulling troops out of Iraq and providing better support for programs that help address poverty. Individuals have options too.

It's a cliché that merits repeating: for Americans, the overwhelming problems faced by poor nations are largely out of sight and out of mind. Everyone can do something to help.

PRACTICAL INFORMATION

- Over 1,500 children die each day of hunger-related disease, one every five seconds. Largely preventable and treatable, malaria kills about one million people annually, and 350 million to 500 million people get the disease each year.

- Nearly one and a half billion people live below the poverty line, earning less than $1.25 per day.

- Over one billion people have no access at all to basic sanitation facilities, even the crudest toilets.

- One in five adults lacks basic literacy skills, 98 percent of them living in developing countries.

- About 1 percent of the federal budget goes to international affairs, versus 20 percent to national defense.

(Sources: Bread for the World, World Watch Institute, National Priorities Project)

WHAT *YOU* CAN DO

Take action on global issues. The Internet has made it possible for us to support international political actions by signing online petitions, sending statements, or having a virtual presence of some other kind. By joining Avaaz.org (listed in the recommended resources) you can participate in progressive grassroots actions worldwide.

Give a percentage of your total yearly contributions to international groups. That way, you'll be sure to support international organizations, such as those we have listed.

Volunteer Abroad. Programs allow you to spend a short time—a few days or weeks—assisting in developing countries, or years at a time. Five million Americans took part in vacations involving volunteerism in 2007.

Tell your Representatives in Congress to support the United Nations' Millennium Development Goals. Joining other wealthy nations, President George W. Bush committed the United States to, among other things, cutting international poverty and hunger in half by 2015. But U.S. funding has not matched the pledge.

RECOMMENDED RESOURCES

Avaaz, www.avaaz.org, is a multi-issue, Internet-based advocacy organization that focuses on international issues. It sends e-mails in 13 languages, mobilizing over 3 million members to take action in response to major global issues and events wherever they happen worldwide.

Doctors without Borders, http://doctorswithoutborders.org, provides medical and other support internationally.

Free Language, http://freelanguage.org, offers resources to learn a language for free.

Globe Aware, www.globeaware.org, offers vacations abroad with a volunteer component.

Heifer International, www.heifer.org, offers families in developing countries the chance to lift themselves out of poverty through gifts of livestock and agricultural training, which provides them with food and income. Donating on behalf of your friends and family makes a nice gift.

Kiva, www.kiva.org, allows you to support specific entrepreneurs in developing countries who are in need of funding for their local businesses.

Oxfam International, www.oxfam.org, works internationally to produce a just world without poverty.

Peace Corps, www.peacecorps.gov, is a U.S. government program that places volunteers in developing countries to work on projects involving health, agriculture, business, education, and more.

Teach Abroad, www.teachabroad.com/search.cfm, posts teaching jobs from all over the world.

Be the Change

I won't just ask for your vote as a candidate; I will ask for your service and your active citizenship when I am President of the United States. This will not be a call issued in one speech or program; this will be a cause of my presidency.

—Senator Barack Obama, "A Call to Serve,"
speaking to students at Cornell College
on December 5, 2007, Mt. Vernon, IA

[24]

Rescue a Pound Puppy!

We have got to take turns walking the dog.

—President Barack Obama, walking Bo,
the First Dog, on the south lawn
of the White House, April 14, 2009

THE CHALLENGE

President Barack Obama stunned the world by referring to himself as a "mutt" during his first presidential news conference. This led to headlines such as "Obama defies political correctness at first press conference."

But we were thinking, America is a nation of mutts, human and canine, so what's the big deal? The mutt reference was made during a discussion of the presidential dog, promised to President Obama's girls during the campaign. The pooch choice reportedly became a major topic in the Obama household, and we know it was a hot topic at water coolers across America.

It turns out that the Obamas adopted a Portuguese Water Dog. What's a Portuguese Water Dog? you're wondering. Our question exactly. We know it's no mutt.

That's what we were hoping the Obamas would get, because we think it's a perfect metaphor for 21st-century America, and for our future promise as a nation. Mutts are tough, hardworking, innovative, available, disease resistant, and cute. They're also abundant and cheap, like renewable energy.

But you know what? Everyone had an opinion on what kind of dog the president's family should have—and where they should get it. That's fine, and fun, but last we checked, it was their dog choice, not ours. And even the cutest dog won't win over those entrenched right-wing extremists in Congress.

So support President Obama by adopting a dog, any dog. But get a mutt from the shelter if you can.

PRACTICAL INFORMATION

- You don't think any information about adopting a dog is practical for this book? People love dogs. And to be the most effective agent for change you can be, doesn't it help to be happy?

- Consider this: Michael Markarian wrote of "paw-litical pets" on the *Huffington Post*, pointing out that campaigns go to great lengths to "harness pet power." This makes a lot of sense, given the love of pets in America.

- The last election saw the emergence of "Pit Bulls Against Palin" and, if you can believe it, "Mutts for McCain." (Those mutts must have been fat-cat CEOs.) So never dismiss dog power.

- Eighty-eight percent of dog owners trip over their pets, resulting in 240 visits to emergency rooms nationwide every day, according to the Centers for Disease Control and Prevention. There was no information about which breeds are the most dangerous in this regard. In any case, if Obama has his way, all these clumsy pet owners will at least have health insurance!

WHAT *YOU* CAN DO

Adopt a shelter dog. (But please don't name him Obama.)

If you already own a dog, dress it up. Buy a "Mutts for Obama" dog T-shirt. (Don't worry if your dog is a purebred—we're sure it won't object to wearing an Obama T-shirt.)

Buy your dog an Obama scarf at www.thedogvote.com.

Clip any political button to your dog's (or cat's) collar. This gets attention at the dog park, from humans and dogs alike.

Spay/neuter your dog. While there has been great improvement in the numbers of unwanted and abandoned dogs, shelters can still be overwhelmed. Unless you plan on breeding, it is a good option to control the pet population.

RECOMMENDED RESOURCES

Dumb Friends League, www.ddfl.org, is an organization which provides shelter and care for animals.

The Humane Society of the United States, www.hsus.org/pets, provides pet adoption information.

Pets 911, www.pets911.com, lists local dog shelters.

[25]

Inspire Yourself to Stay Involved

If there is anyone out there who still doubts that America is a place where all things are possible; who still wonders if the dream of our founders is alive in our time; who still questions the power of our democracy, tonight is your answer... It's been a long time coming, but tonight, because of what we did on this day, in this election, at this defining moment, change has come to America.

—President-Elect Barack Obama,
election night victory speech, November 4, 2008,
Grant Park, Chicago, IL

THE CHALLENGE

We didn't include "Inspire Yourself" in our initial list of 50 chapters for this book. But when we started writing and rereading the speeches and life story of President Obama, guess what happened? We got inspired.

You may be surprised to know that we're not Obama flunkies. We're skeptical of just about any politician, like most people. Still, his election and his intelligence energized us throughout the campaign. We think Obama is inspiring us as much as ever. After all, here we are listing ways to help him. But as we were writing this book and dedicating more time to listening to President Obama talk about his life and beliefs, we noticed an increase in our own commitment to taking action to promote his vision.

So we add this chapter to encourage you to take a bit of time to get inspired by President Obama and the good things about America. It may help sustain your energy for activism.

PRACTICAL INFORMATION

The simple act of doing something—anything—may inspire you to continue to be involved and do even more. A study by Dr. John Drury, a psychologist at the University of Sussex, suggests that activists enjoy better physical and mental health. Drury told Reuters "the take-home message from this research therefore might be that people should get more involved in campaigns, struggles, and social movements, not only in the wider interest of social change but also for their own personal good." Drury attributes the activists' positive mental states to the happiness and even euphoria derived from collective action.

WHAT *YOU* CAN DO

Visit Washington DC. What better time to go to Washington and focus on all the positive aspects of our country? Read about Lincoln as you take in the Lincoln Memorial at night—one of President Obama's favorite places, which he discussed in the final paragraphs of *The Audacity of Hope*. Go to the White House and the Capitol. And while you're there, you can visit your representatives and tell them to support Obama or else. Public tours of the White House are available for groups of 10 or more people. Requests must be submitted through a member of Congress from your state.

Watch a few of the president's best speeches. Search YouTube for some of Obama's greatest speeches, including the one he gave at the 2004 Democratic National Convention or his inaugural address.

Make a point to watch unedited videos of Obama's current speeches. It's less inspirational to watch a sound bite or read a quote in an article. Check out his full statements online, particularly when he's answering questions. His thoughtfulness inspires.

Read Barack Obama's *Dreams from My Father*. It's still hard for us to believe that the guy who wrote this book is now President of the United States. His sensitivity and honesty emerge from the writing in this book more than in any of his other writings.

Watch a video of President Bush. Yes. Even if it's just for five minutes. There's nothing like a glimpse of past mistakes to make us thankful for what we have.

RECOMMENDED RESOURCES

TheDistrict.com, www.thedistrict.com, is an excellent Web site with information on all aspects of visiting Washington DC.

Indie Bound, www.indiebound.org, supports independent businesses around the country. You can look up local independent bookstores to visit and buy a book about the president.

Progressive Rags, www.progressiverags.com, sells Obama posters and buttons.

The Progressive Revolution: How the Best in America Came to Be (Hoboken, N.J.: Wiley, 2009) is an inspiring read by Michael Lux that describes how progressives have forged the ideals for all of us.

YouTube, www.youtube.com, lets you view Obama's speeches.

[26]

Plant Your Own Garden

I wanted to be able to bring what I learned to a broader base of people. And what better way to do it than to plant a vegetable garden in the south lawn of the White House? For urban dwellers who have no backyards, the country's one million community gardens can also play an important role.

—*First Lady Michelle Obama,*
The White House, March 19, 2009, Washington DC

THE CHALLENGE

For any of you who don't think change can happen in America, think about this: Michelle Obama has already attacked the White House lawn with a shovel.

"What Michelle and the kids and the crew did the other day was to drive a shovel right into the heart of that American icon: the lawn," columnist Ellen Goodman wrote. "They literally took the most pampered lawn in America, dumped it in the wheelbarrow and carted it away."

The Obamas' decision to replace a 1,100-square-foot patch of grass on the south lawn with a White House kitchen garden shouldn't be dismissed merely as symbolic. Urban gardening is connected to a way of thinking about health and the environment that has the power to transform the world—not just the taste buds of kids like Sasha and Malia.

Eating food that's grown nearby eliminates pollution. For example, the Natural Resources Defense Council calculates that ships and trucks carrying grapes from places like Chile to the Port of Los Angeles release over 7,000 tons of global-warming pollution each year. And that's just grapes transported to the Port of Los Angeles.

When you buy locally grown foods, you're often supporting small farmers, who don't use pesticides and offer an alternative to the giant corporations that dominate agriculture globally.

We know that in the end, the farm bill matters more than any garden, even the Obamas' plot with 55 different kinds of veggies. But why should that stop you from planting one? At least embrace the notion of "planting a garden" as a metaphor for better health (yours and the Earth's). As Michelle Obama said, "You can begin in your own cupboard, by eliminating processed food, trying to cook a meal a little more often, trying to incorporate more fruits and vegetables."

PRACTICAL INFORMATION

- Over a quarter of global-warming gas emissions are associated with America's food system.

- If Americans had one vegetarian meal per week, we'd cut emissions of carbon dioxide by the same amount as we'd eliminate by taking five million cars off the road.

- The research on food and the environment is evolving, and it's important to keep learning about the most environmentally friendly ways to grow food, even if it's not local.

- The benefits of eating local foods range from better taste and freshness to better community connections and preservation of open space.

(Sources: Mother Jones, Environmental Defense Fund)

WHAT *YOU* CAN DO

Find a community garden. There are about a million community gardens in our country—filled with great produce and great communities of people. You can get your own plot or share.

Plant your own plot. Assemble information you need from our list of resources. Try a variety of plants, which makes it more likely you'll have success with something.

Choose a sunny place with good soil. Specific tips for gardening—when to plant, what to plant, and how to avoid pitfalls along the way—vary according to where you live. But for best results, you need an area with full sun and rich soil.

Try outdoor pots. If a garden is too ambitious for you, get some seeds or seedlings and plant them in pots. Grow herbs, peppers, tomatoes, all kinds of great stuff on your porch or front steps. (An indoor windowsill works for herbs, too.)

Join community-supported agriculture. In some areas, you can support a local farm by buying part of its annual harvest.

Shop at farmers' markets. This is a great way to connect with neighbors and eat healthier food.

Read labels. An easy way to start educating yourself about food is to find out where your food comes from and what's in it.

Buy local food. Even some big chain supermarkets advertise food that's locally grown.

Ask for locally grown food. Ask your grocer to carry local products.

RECOMMENDED RESOURCES

American Community Gardening Association, www.communitygarden.org, lists community gardens by area.

Eat Well, www.eatwellguide.com, helps you find sustainably raised food and other products near you.

Local Harvest, www.localharvest.org, is a national directory of community-supported agriculture, farmers' markets, and other sustainable food sources and products.

Michael Pollan, www.michaelpollan.com, has written some of the best books on the food industry and local farming.

Natural Resources Defense Council, www.nrdc.org/health/foodmiles/default .asp, allows you to visit its Web site and calculate how far your food has traveled to reach your table.

Rodale Institute, www.rodaleinstitute.org/organic_kids, sponsors gardening workshops, provides online information about nutrition, and offers ideas for what families and kids can do to learn about organic gardening and healthy food.

[27]

Get News That's
Truly Fair and Balanced

If people are paying attention, then we get good government and good leadership. And when we get lazy as a democracy, and civically start taking shortcuts, then it results in bad government and politics.

—Senator Barack Obama,
"A Different Kind of Politics?"
Newsweek, *September 25, 2006*

THE CHALLENGE

To understand America, we need to do more than tune in to National Public Radio and pretend the rest of the media world doesn't exist.

You should try to be connected to the news consumed by most people—TV news and daily newspapers. We're not saying your news diet should be dictated by large media corporations. We just don't think you should ignore the mainstream media, if you want to stay in touch with our country.

To try to understand what's really going on, it's best to consume a variety of news, from different sources. The Internet makes this easy.

PRACTICAL INFORMATION

- Only 15 percent of Americans say their main source of campaign news is the Internet. Although 44 percent of adults go online for political news and information, television is the number one source of campaign news for 60 percent of Americans, eclipsing newspapers (12 percent) and all other sources. For news in general, U.S. citizens primarily watch local TV news shows.

- Women comprise about half the population but they own just 6 percent of TV and radio stations. And over 80 percent of station managers are male. Large corporations dominate the media industry, including television, newspapers, radio, books, and film.

- People aged 18 to 24 watch the least amount of television, compared to other age groups in America.

- From 2007 to 2008, visits to top newspaper Web sites increased by 200 percent.

(Sources: Pew Research Center for People and the Press, Pew Internet and American Life Project, Free Press, New Organizing Institute)

WHAT *YOU* CAN DO

Avoid the media rut. Keep checking out different news sources. Listen to conservative talk radio for a while and then try a community radio station. Check in with different blogs. Switch from alternative weeklies to other free print publications.

Find local blogs. We've listed great national news and information sources, but you should be a regular consumer of the best local blogs in your community as well. (For a list of local bloggers, visit www.leftyblogs.com.)

Explore new links. New and improved sources of information, particularly about emerging issues, sprout up daily on the Web. Look for links on the "blog rolls" of your favorite blog or in articles you read online. Take a moment to click on these links.

Read your local daily newspaper. It probably still tracks local political news like no other source.

Get the international perspective. In a globalized economy it's important to check global news. Foreign newsgroups can also have good viewpoints on U.S. politics. Try to catch up weekly with the BBC (http://news.bbc.co.uk) which offers analysis and blogs.

RECOMMENDED RESOURCES

Blogs you will want to check out include DailyKos.com, TalkLeft.com, TalkingPointsMemo.com, and many others.

The Center for Independent Media, www.newjournalist.org, runs a network of online news sites, among other things.

Google Alerts can allow you to track any person (including yourself) or issue in the news by logging onto www.google.com and clicking on "Google Alerts." Follow the step-by-step instructions to track the news you choose.

The Media Consortium, www.themediaconsortium.org, is a network of independent media outlets.

Progressive magazines such as *Mother Jones*, the *Nation*, *Progressive*, *Utne Reader*, *Yes!*, and *Z Magazine* also have Web sites.

Radio programs that you might want to listen to include Air America, Democracy Now!, and National Public Radio.

Television has options as well. CurrentTV, www.current.com, is a global television network that gives you the opportunity to create and influence what airs on TV. Free Speech TV, www.freespeechtv. org, is a progressive television station. LinkTV, www.linktv.org, is a national network using digital technology to offers news, current events, and culture stories. The Public Broadcasting Service, www .pbs.org, is a nonprofit public broadcasting television service with 354 member TV stations in the United States.

Web-based news sources include Alternet.org, BuzzFlash.org, Common Dreams.org, HuffingtonPost.com, and Truthout.org. These Web-based organizations offer original and previously published commentary and news reporting.

Beltway political dailies. Good options are *The Hill* (http://thehill.com), *Hotline On Call* (http://hotlineoncall.nationaljournal.com), and *Roll Call* (www.rollcall.com). These also offer breaking news alerts via e-mail. *Congressional Quarterly* (www.cq.com) is one of the best for insight into Congressional politics. The *Washington Post* (www .washingtonpost.com) and the *New York Times* (www.nytimes.com) offer in-depth politics sections daily and feature optional alerts to keep you up-to-the-minute.

[28]

Use Public Transportation

What we need, then, is a smart transportation system equal to the needs of the 21st century. A system that reduces travel times and increases mobility. A system that reduces congestion and boosts productivity. A system that reduces destructive emissions and creates jobs. What we're talking about is a vision for high-speed rail in America. Imagine boarding a train in the center of a city. No racing to an airport and across a terminal, no delays, no sitting on the tarmac, no lost luggage, no taking off your shoes. Imagine whisking through towns at speeds over 100 miles an hour, walking only a few steps to public transportation, and ending up just blocks from your destination. Imagine what a great project that would be to rebuild America.

—President Barack Obama, remarking on his vision
for high-speed rail in America, April 16, 2009,
The White House, Washington DC

THE CHALLENGE

President Obama knows that a major way to stimulate our economy is by investing in our transportation infrastructure and in cleaner forms of transportation.

You can help promote both goals by patronizing your local public transportation system. Whether you take the bus, light-rail, or high-speed rail, you'll be doing the planet and your community a favor. And in the future, your high-speed light-rail options will be increased dramatically, thanks to the plan to build high-speed rail in the economic stimulus package.

PRACTICAL INFORMATION

- Riding public transportation and living with one car in a household can save an individual $8,670 a year, based on the April 8, 2009 national average gas price and the unreserved monthly parking rate.

- Use of public transportation has risen 38 percent since 1995.

- Riding a public bus is 91 times safer than car travel.

- For every $10 million invested in public transportation, more than $15 million is saved in transportation costs to both highway and public transportation users.

- If one in 10 Americans used public transportation regularly, the United States reliance on foreign oil could be cut by more than 40 percent—the amount we import from Saudi Arabia each year.

(Sources: PublicTransportation.org, Central Midlands Regional Transportation Authority, Transportation Choices Coalition)

WHAT *YOU* CAN DO

Commit to taking public transportation at least one more day a week than you do now. If you don't already use public transportation, this is a great way to get more familiar with the system in your community. If you do use public transportation regularly, you're further promoting transportation infrastructure as well as decreasing oil dependence and emissions. Plus, it's a lot more relaxing to sit on a bus than fight your way through gridlock.

Ask your public transportation agency to upgrade to biodiesel or electric. Many cities throughout America are slowly phasing out their diesel buses in favor of biodiesel and electric forms of transportation. Let your transit agency know that you want to patronize them and that it is important to you that they take steps to decrease their emissions.

Buy bulk tickets or a monthly pass. By purchasing more than one ticket at a time, you usually decrease your per ticket expenditure for public transportation. Also, once you have them, you'll be inspired to use them.

RECOMMENDED RESOURCES

American Public Transportation Association, www.apta.com, provides facts about transit and other transit-related information.

Public Transportation Takes Us There, www.publictransportation.org, offers information about public transportation, as well as ways to determine what options are available in your area.

Transportation Choices Coalition, www.transportationchoices.org, has good information on public transport.

[29]

Support Socially
Responsible Businesses

This is a much broader issue than Wal-Mart, but I think the battle to engage Wal-Mart and force them to examine their own corporate values and what their policies and approaches are to their workers and how they are going to be good corporate citizens, I think, is absolutely vital. If Costco can do that, it means Wal-Mart can do it. And if Wal-Mart does it, then what we're going to see is other companies recognizing that they have some obligations not only to their shareholders but also to their stakeholders, and that's workers and communities in which they're located.

—Senator Barack Obama, "Obama Says Wal-Mart
Is Part of Necessary Debate on Pay and Benefits,"
Associated Press, November 16, 2006

THE CHALLENGE

In a tangible way, we vote every time we spend or invest a dollar. Maybe our individual expenditures and investments don't mean much, but when you combine your dollars with those of the millions of others who want to make a difference and help Obama succeed, we're talking serious economic power. And economic power translates into political power. Who can glance at the political world for more than a nanosecond and argue with that?

So we should support companies that reflect our ideals—the ones that support Obama or treat their workers ethically or act in a socially responsible manner.

Obama divested his investment in a mutual fund in 2007 after learning that it included an oil company which was profiting from its oil fields in Sudan as hundreds of thousands of innocent people were killed in the Darfur region of that country. We're amazed how few of us actually link our political beliefs with our expenditures—even though it's one of the easiest ways in this book to support President Obama and his campaign for change.

PRACTICAL INFORMATION

- Being socially responsible attracts customers. "Being socially responsible" is the strongest factor affecting brand loyalty for 35 percent of consumers, versus lower prices (20 percent), easily available (20 percent), product prestige (3 percent), and even quality (6 percent).

- Sustainable companies have been outperforming their competitors during the recent economic crisis.

- Socially responsible mutual funds received Morningstar's highest ranking more often than mutual funds generally.

  (Sources: Goldman Sachs, A. T. Kearney, Morningstar)

WHAT *YOU* CAN DO

Support companies that fight climate change. Climate Counts is an organization that rates companies and ranks them against their competitors according to how much they're doing to fight global warming. Go to www.climatecounts.org and download "pocket guide."

Don't patronize these companies, whose founders or chair-people are big time conservative donors: Applebee's Restaurants, Best Buy, Dell Computers, Dominos Pizza, Home Depot, Kellogg's, PepsiCo (which includes Frito-Lay, Gatorade, and Tropicana), Pier 1 Stores, Urban Outfitters, and Wal-Mart.

Join boycotts of companies that are doing bad things. For example, boycott Exxon-Mobil until it supports the Kyoto Accord. Boycott McDonald's until it removes its restaurant in Guantanamo. Boycott General Motors until they stop suing to reverse California's tough global warming regulations.

Join the Progressive Book Club. This company's mission is to "find the books and showcase the ideas that can change our nation for the better." When you buy a book, you select an organization that will receive a donation. Books are offered at a discount, and a board of leading progressives selects featured titles. (www.progressivebookclub.com)

Use Working Assets' cell phone or long-distance phone service. When you do, a portion of the charges is donated to progressive organizations. Over $60 million has been donated since 1985. (www.workingassets.com)

RECOMMENDED RESOURCES

Americans for Informed Democracy, www.aidemocracy.org/download /divestment.pdf, has produced a guide on how to pressure an institution to divest its holdings from bad corporations.

Boston Phoenix, www.bostonphoenix.com/boston/news_features/top/documents/buyerbeware_bar1.pdf, provides a list of companies that support far-right-wing causes.

Business Leaders for Social Responsibility, www.bsr.org, is an organization of businesses that implement socially responsible programs.

Corporate Accountability International, www.stopcorporateabuse.org, challenges abuse by corporations worldwide.

Feeling Blue Seeing Red, www.feelingblueseeingred.org, tracks corporate boycotts, among other things.

Media Transparency, www.mediatransparency.org, is a good way to follow the conservative money trail, especially in the media and policy worlds.

Socially Responsible Investing, www.socialinvest.org and www.socialfunds.com, provides resources and tools to help you select investments and mutual funds that are socially responsible.

Social Venture Network, www.svn.org, is a network of progressive businesspeople.

WakeUpWalMart, www.wakeupwalmart.com, is a grassroots campaign to change Wal-Mart and hold the company accountable.

Wal-Mart Watch, www.walmartwatch.com, is a public education campaign to challenge Wal-Mart to become a better employer, neighbor, and corporate citizen.

[30]

Green Your Home for the Earth's Sake

Environmentalism is not an upper-income issue, it's not a white issue,
it's not a black issue, it's not a South or a North or an East or a West
issue. It's an issue that all of us have a stake in.

—Senator Barack Obama, speaking at
a League of Conservation Voters rally
on July 27, 2004, Boston, MA

THE CHALLENGE

For David Akerson, energy independence starts at home.

First, there's his tiny VW bug. His kids are sick of its french-fry
smell, but more important than the odor is the fact that it runs on
recycled veggie oil, dumped from the frying vats of local restaurants.
Then there's his solar-equipped house, his beehive, his organic garden,
and his compost pile that actually works, instead of just attracting mice
and stinking up the yard and feeding the squirrels. His home has tons
of insulation, super energy-efficient Energy Star appliances, airtight
windows, and more.

Akerson loves to talk about bringing not only cloth bags to the
grocery store, but jars as well, to hold bulk foods and thereby eliminate

packaging. This simple act is so rare and confusing that the checkout staff will sometimes give him his bulk brown rice for free, because they don't know how to factor in the weight of the reusable jar.

Akerson's carbon-footprint obsession might get hard to live with. But if we're going to live at all on Earth, and if we want to be the change Obama wants, maybe we should all try to be more like Akerson.

PRACTICAL INFORMATION

- For every 10 degrees that you lower the temperature of your water heater, you save $6–$10 per year. You'll save 5–10 percent on your heating bill by turning your heat down five degrees at night. Insulating and weatherizing your home can save 20 percent on heating costs, and one compact fluorescent bulb can save about $40.

- The Clinton administration pushed through a regulation requiring air conditioners and heat pumps to be 30 percent more efficient. This single regulation will keep 51 million metric tons of carbon out of the air. That's like eliminating 34 million cars from America's roads.

- Americans are just 4 percent of the global population, but we produce 25 percent of carbon dioxide, the major global-warming gas.

- We have the technology to cut energy use drastically. We just need to put these technologies to use.

(Sources: American Council for an Economic Efficient Economy, Department of Energy, Natural Resources Defense Council)

WHAT *YOU* CAN DO

Lower the temperature setting of your water heater to 120 degrees or lower. And buy an insulated jacket for it to reduce the energy required to maintain the water at a high temperature.

Turn down your thermostat to 68 degrees or lower in the winter and 78 degrees or higher in the summer. And lower the temperature by 5 degrees at night. (A programmable thermostat makes this easy.)

Use cold water in your washing machine. How cool is that?

Switch to compact fluorescent light bulbs.

Add insulation to your attic. This is the most cost-effective first step you can take to making your home more energy efficient. You'd think it might be insulating windows, but it's not.

Purchase Energy Star appliances. Energy Star is a ratings system used to help citizens save energy using efficient services and products, including home appliances. Energy Star is a joint program of the Department of Energy and the Environmental Protection Agency.

Use a clothesline whenever possible, not a dryer. If using a dryer, use a full load and clean the lint trap.

Turn computers off at night, and make the extra effort to turn off unnecessary lighting.

RECOMMENDED RESOURCES

50 Simple Things, www.50simplethings.com/resources/things_you_can_do, is the companion Web site for the classic book *50 Simple Things You Can Do to Save the Earth*.

American Council for an Energy-Efficient Economy, www.aceee.org, is dedicated to advancing energy efficiency and has an abundance of suggestions for consumers about home energy use and savings.

Energy Star, www.energystar.gov, lists energy-efficient appliances and offers other energy-saving advice.

Home Energy Saver, http://hes.lbl.gov, lets you enter details about your home and gives you tips on how to save energy.

An Inconvenient Truth, www.climatecrisis.net, is the Web site connected to Al Gore's movie of the same name. Click on "Take Action."

Spend More Time with Your Kids

In the end, there is no program or policy that can substitute for a mother or father who will attend those parent/teacher conferences, or help with homework after dinner, or turn off the TV, put away the video games, and read to their child. I speak to you not just as a president, but as a father when I say that responsibility for our children's education must begin at home.

—President Barack Obama,
addressing a joint session of Congress,
February 24, 2009, Washington DC

THE CHALLENGE

We both have kids, and we know how crazy they can be and how insane family life can get with them, even if they stay healthy for three consecutive days. Then there's the party for the soccer team, teacher appreciation day, the day care play, and the fall festival. And you've got to love summer vacation.

The temptation to plug the kids into the TV and fall asleep on the couch is huge, and we need to support each other to resist it, or at least not overdo it.

On the bright side, research shows that Americans are actually spending more time with their kids than they did in the 1960s, in part because dads are stepping up. We're also sacrificing things we did more of in the 1960s, like sleep.

Still, President Obama, who appears to need very little sleep, encourages us to spend more quality time with our children. You don't need researchers to say that it helps kids in all kinds of ways, emotionally and academically, not to mention the sense of well-being it can give to parents. The president himself has breakfast with the family most mornings—as well as dinner when he's not traveling. That's what Michelle Obama told *People* magazine.

And Obama is making it more practical for parents to afford to spend time with their kids, by supporting flexible work arrangements, a higher minimum wage, affordable college education, programs for parents with young children, and more.

PRACTICAL INFORMATION

- Mothers spend 14 hours per week of focused time with their kids (playing, reading, eating) versus 10 hours in 1965. To free up time, they're cutting back on housework (down by 40 percent over 38 years) and sleep, among other things—and they're multitasking. Married mothers spend about 50 hours per week of focused and unfocused time with their kids versus 47 hours in 1975. For fathers, the figure is 33 hours versus 21.

- Forty-eight percent of preschool children are cared for by a relative, friend, sibling, or mother while she works.

- About 68 percent of children under 18 years old live with married parents, 23 percent live with only their mothers, 3 percent with only their fathers.

- About a quarter of the U.S. population is children under 18.

(Sources: University of Maryland, Federal Interagency Forum on Child and Family Statistics)

WHAT *YOU* CAN DO

Go on a picnic. Avoid the in-house distractions, pack some simple food, and go to the park. It can be across the street and you can feel like you're worlds away from the stress of the house. If preparing food seems daunting, try take-out.

Schedule it. One of the best ways to spend relaxed time with your kids—or your relatives' kids—is to put it on your regular schedule, like you would a weekly meeting at work. So you might take a look at your schedule and slot in dedicated kid time, not just to being at home or helping with homework but doing something together that's fun.

Read to your kids. Imagine if our entire country did it. Try hanging out at the library.

Cook together. Baking is the best, but kids of all ages love to mess up the kitchen.

Plant a veggie garden together. Studies actually show that kids like vegetables more if they're grown in a family garden. This even applies to homegrown beets! Plus, it's fun, even for small children. We like to plant the biggest vegetables possible for dramatic impact. But planting small herbs or tomatoes in pots on the porch or in the windowsill is great too. (See our chapter, "Plant Your Own Garden.")

Play board games. Michelle and Barack Obama reportedly do it. It's an easy way to bond.

Start traditions. Kids love to do the same thing year after year. Try harvesting carrots from your garden on Thanksgiving or eating Chinese food on the Chinese New Year, or returning to the same camping spot each year.

Write a letter for what you want for your kids. Writing down what you want for your children may help clarify your goals and aspirations. Read Obama's own inspirational letter to his two girls by searching on the Internet for "What I want for you" in *Parade* magazine.

RECOMMENDED RESOURCES

Babybug, www.cricketmag.com, is just one of the many magazines for kids from Carus Publishing.

Invest in Kids, www.investinkids.ca, provides helpful points on how to spend quality time with your kids from birth to age five.

MomsRising, www.momsrising.org, bring motherhood and family issues to the forefront of the country's awareness.

Mothers Acting Up, www.mothersactingup.org, is a mother-led organization that offers programs including Take Action: The Mother Agenda.

MyBarackObama, www.barackobama.com/issues/family, covers President Obama's positions on various issues relating to children and families.

Schoolhouse Rock!, those short musical cartoons that used to be shown on Saturday mornings, are now available on DVD and even iTunes. They made it fun to learn grammar, science, economics, history, mathematics, and civics. Watch the classic "I'm Just a Bill" on YouTube.

You Are Your Child's First Teacher, by Rahima Baldwin Dancy, gives suggestions on what you can do with your child from birth to age six.

[32]

Quit Smoking

My wife wisely indicated that this is a potentially stressful situation, running for president. She wanted to lay down a very clear marker that she wants me healthy.

—*Senator Barack Obama,*
"Obama Tries to Kick the Habit" in the
St. Petersburg Times, *February 6, 2007*

THE CHALLENGE

Heart disease, emphysema, lung cancer, oral cancer. These are the well-known risks for the habitual cigarette smoker—including President Obama—if he doesn't find a way to kick the habit for good.

Is the president still a smoker? In an interview on "Meet the Press" just weeks after he was elected, the president said we would not see any violations of the White House's anti-smoking rule. Does this mean he's quit? We don't know for sure, but we want to believe that the answer is yes. So how does this chapter make the cut in a book that regards our president in such high esteem? Well, we know it's not easy to quit, and we're sure President Obama wants to, if he hasn't already.

He's a smart guy and he knows how bad it is: The toll smoking takes not only on human health, but also on the pocketbook, is well documented. It's estimated by the Centers for Disease Control and

Prevention that cigarette smoking was responsible for $167 billion in annual health-related economic losses in the United States ($92 billion in lost productivity, and $75 billion in direct medical costs), or about $3,561 per adult smoker, just from 1997 to 2001.

And how about the toll on the environment? Trillions of poison-laden, slow-to-biodegrade cigarette butts litter our streets and highways.

So you see why we want to believe President Obama did quit. Because there are so many good reasons, for the country and for smokers themselves, to do so.

PRACTICAL INFORMATION

- The five major U.S. cigarette companies account for 90 percent of the cigarettes sold in a given year. Between them they rake in around $15 billion per year. That's just less than twice what America spends on the Environmental Protection Agency.

- There are about 1.1 billion smokers in the world. Every eight seconds there is a tobacco-related death somewhere on this planet, which adds up to more than 4 million deaths per year. And American youths are still picking up cigarettes at a rate of 3,000 new smokers per day. More than 440,000 Americans per year fall victim to diseases caused by smoking.

- A major legislative initiative finally passed to place regulatory power over the tobacco industry in the hands of the Federal Food and Drug Administration. One would think this would have happened long ago. But Big Tobacco has fought hard to keep this from happening. Contact your lawmakers and thank them for passing this landmark legislation.

(Sources: Centers for Disease Control and Prevention, U.S. Department of Agriculture, World Health Organization, Maxwell Report)

WHAT *YOU* CAN DO

Read up on the physical and mental effects of nicotine withdrawal so you know what to expect when the time comes.

Make a list of the reasons you want to quit smoking. Carry it with you at all times.

Keep a quitting journal where you record your visions of the benefits of being a non-smoker, and eventually track your progress. When the going gets rough, you can look back on week one and see how far you've come.

Choose your quitting method according to your needs, whether it is cold turkey, nicotine replacement, herbal remedy, hypnotism, or some other way. Don't be afraid to ask for help and check out some of the Web sites we've listed.

Add up how much money you spend on cigarettes per week, and save it up. After a month of successful smoke-free living, buy yourself a nice gift.

Fight off nicotine cravings with deep breathing exercises. This really works. You'd be surprised.

RECOMMENDED RESOURCES

The American Cancer Society, www.cancer.org, has a very comprehensive guide for quitting smoking. It features a particularly detailed section on nicotine addiction with fascinating illustrations, as well as many other helpful resources.

Campaign for Tobacco-Free Kids, www.tobaccofreekids.org, has up-to-date information on how you can affect legislation to reduce the power of the tobacco lobby and the harms of tobacco, as well as statistics of the toll of tobacco in each state.

The Centers for Disease Control and Prevention, www.cdc.gov/tobacco, offers ideas on how to quit smoking on its Web site. Also of interest here is a host of damning information about the tobacco industry and its practices, as well as statistics that should be enough to push any smoker to kick the habit.

National Cancer Institute, www.smokefree.gov, has a Web site that's rich with information on the benefits and methods of quitting smoking, with a handy PDF you can download and carry with you.

Amplify Your Voice for Change

I'm asking you to believe. Not just in my ability to bring about real change in Washington . . . . I'm asking you to believe in yours.

—*President Barack Obama, www.barackobama.com*

[33]

Take Back the Flag

"We hold these truths to be self-evident, that all men are created equal, that they are endowed by their Creator with certain unalienable Rights, that among these are Life, Liberty and the pursuit of Happiness." Those simple words are our starting point as Americans; they describe not only the foundation of our government but the substance of our common creed.

—*Senator Barack Obama, "Values,"* The Audacity of Hope

THE CHALLENGE

In *The Audacity of Hope*, President Obama recalls how Democratic Senator Robert Byrd would pull out a pocked-sized Constitution to "wave in the midst of a debate." The right wing has been so effective at claiming patriotism as a conservative virtue, as opposed to a progressive one, that the sight of Byrd waving a mini-Constitution rightfully struck then-Senator Obama as a beautiful thing.

And it would be even more beautiful if more of us were equipped with Constitutions in our pockets, for waving in the lunchroom at the office or for brandishing during a political chat with a swing voter. And we can do this for free—at the expense of far right-wingers—while supplies last.

The ultra-conservative Heritage Foundation will give you a free "pocket Constitution" when you sign up for its online newsletters. So by ordering one, you get to 1) deplete the Heritage Foundation of a small amount of money, 2) review the kind of information an organization like the Heritage Foundation is distributing, and 3), most importantly, own a mini-Constitution of your very own. Here's the link to get yours today: www.heritage.org/morningbell. (Other sources are listed in the resource section.)

And if you don't have pockets or don't like carrying things for whatever reason, you'll find more you can do to reclaim the flag, like fly it or teach civics.

PRACTICAL INFORMATION

- About two-thirds of Americans fly a flag at home, at work, or on their car.

- Seventy-three percent of Republicans say they display the flag at home, at work, or on their car, compared with 63 percent of independents and 55 percent of Democrats.

  (Source: Pew Research Center)

WHAT *YOU* CAN DO

Fly a flag from your house. Be sure to take the flag inside during the evening, if you fly it on a regular basis. If that's too much, consider flying the flag on special occasions, like Independence Day, other holidays, or in response to current events. Our neighbor has some fun by flying the American flag most of the time, but also an Earth flag on Earth Day, a green one on St. Patrick's Day, a United Nations flag on occasion, and more.

Place a flag bumper sticker or window decal on your car. It's easy to do and effective, especially if you have an Obama sticker on one side of your bumper and a flag sticker on the other.

Buy a flag lapel pin. One of the lowest points in the last election came in October 2007, when Obama's patriotism was questioned because he had stopped wearing an American flag lapel pin. Having one can be useful for special occasions. While President Obama had once told *Time* magazine, "Sometimes I wear it, sometimes I don't" you now seldom see him without it.

Get a pocket constitution. It's free from the Heritage Foundation, as mentioned earlier. Posters of the Constitution are also available. You can also buy a mini—Declaration of Independence or download it on your smart phone and wave as appropriate.

Teach Civics. Consider offering to teach civics at a school—or at least force it on your own kids or relatives.

As we begin our fourth century as a nation, it is easy to take the extraordinary nature of America for granted. But it is our responsibility as Americans and as parents to instill that history in our children, both at home and at school. The loss of quality civic education from so many of our classrooms has left too many young Americans without the most basic knowledge of who our forefathers are, or what they did, or the significance of the founding documents that bear their names.

—*Senator Barack Obama,*
"The America We Love,"
June 30, 2008, Independence, MO

RECOMMENDED RESOURCES

National Center for Constitutional Studies, www.nccs.net/us_constitution
.html, will ship you a pocket Constitution for free when you send
an envelope with $0.59 postage to NCCS, 37777 W. Juniper Rd.,
Malta, ID, 83342. (In case the Heritage Foundation runs out.)

Liberty Day, www.libertyday.org, is a non-profit, non-partisan volunteer
effort to educate Americans about the Declaration of Independence
and the U.S. Constitution and has pocket-size copies for 50 cents.
The group also offers volunteer speakers and teachers throughout
the country.

The True Patriot, www.truepat.org, is a concise book by progressives Eric
Liu and Nick Hanauer, who recapture patriotism and inspire.

U.S. Constitution Online, www.usconstitution.net, is all about the U.S.
Constitution, including teaching guides for kids of varying ages.
You can also use this site to pull up the text on your cell phone.

[34]

Make a Statement on the Streets

It goes to show you how one voice can change a room. And if one voice can change a room, it can change a city. And if it can change a city, it can change a state. And if it can change a state, it can change a nation. And if it can change a nation, it can change the world.

—*Senator Barack Obama,*
June 1, 2008, Corn Palace, Mitchell, SD

THE CHALLENGE

"Fired up, ready to go!"

That's the chant that President Obama was referring to when he said a single voice changed the energy level in a room full of people. It came from Edith Childs, who was just another person in the crowd listening to Obama. She's the one who succeeded in getting everyone fired up during an otherwise cold and forgettable morning, at a time in 2008 when Obama's Presidential campaign was sliding back, not forward. She just started chanting, and others began smiling and getting energized, including Obama.

It was a short moment in a long campaign, but it's the kind of story community organizers love, because we're always looking for the next way to get people fired up. Life can be depressing enough, and on top of it are things like the military industrial complex that needs to be controlled. So you can't blame people for feeling apathetic in the face of it all. We all need to be inspired somehow to move forward.

As it turns out, Childs's "Fired up, ready to go!" chant is famous in Greenwood, South Carolina, and it works repeatedly. It's not the kind of thing, obviously, that's going to sustain a campaign or eliminate apathy, but it's part of the mix, even if it's a small part. And the small things you can do as an individual add up. That's why you should see your car's clean bumper as an opportunity to make a statement. Ditto for your windshield. Or even the intersection of two big streets in town.

When you start looking, everyday life is actually a series of opportunities to make a statement, to raise your voice from your car, your lawn, your house, you name it.

PRACTICAL INFORMATION

- Local laws vary when it comes to signs—waving them on the street, placing them on your lawn, where you're allowed to hold them while you stand. Check with the police in advance to avoid breaking the law.

- If you can't find the T-shirt you want, you can make a few yourself. Consider selling them on CaféPress.com, which lets you get into the tchotchke business with very little money down.

WHAT *YOU* CAN DO

Get a yard sign. Depending on the zoning laws in your area, you can have a yard sign up in your front lawn year-round. Or you can have a sign in a prominent window of your home.

Politicize your clothes or your car. T-shirts, buttons, neckties, hats—you can make a statement with what you wear. Or drive.

If you're in love with your clean bumper, try erasable window markers or a yard sign or poster in your car window. Electrostatic signs also work.

Wear a sandwich board. You attach the top corners of two rectangular signs together with rope. Put the ropes over your shoulders and one sheet of cardboard in front of you and the other on your back, creating a sandwich with you in the middle.

Fly a banner from a plane. Businesses in many cities fly airplanes with banners trailing behind them. You can put your message there and ask for a discount on a slow day.

Wave a sign on a street corner. You see people doing this on election day. It gets attention any time. If you've got an animal costume lying around, or want to buy one online, you can make a bigger splash. For example, if your senator is balking at supporting Obama, rent an ostrich costume and make a sign saying your senator has his or her "head in the sand" about the economy.

Place a sign on a bridge over a highway. This is an easy way to get a lot of attention, but make sure it's legal where you live. If so, tell radio traffic reporters in advance that you're going to do it, and maybe you'll get a bit of media attention too.

RECOMMENDED RESOURCES

YouTube, www.youtube.com, has the footage of Obama talking about Edith Childs's chant. Put "Obama fired up" in the search box.

Freeway Blogger, www.freewayblogger.com/howto.htm, encourages individuals to express themselves politically on freeway overpasses. (Check laws in your area.)

Prochoice America, www.prochoiceamerica.org, has produced a good fact sheet on how to wave signs on street corners. Look under "Choice Action Center menu"and click on "Take Action." Scroll down to bulleted list and you'll find out how to hold a "honk and wave."

The Question Alliance, is a married couple that holds signs on street corners. See them on YouTube.

[35]

Stage or Attend a Rally, Media Event, or Protest

Of course, precisely because America isn't perfect, precisely because our ideals constantly demand more from us, patriotism can never be defined as loyalty to any particular leader or government or policy. As Mark Twain, that greatest of American satirists and proud son of Missouri, once wrote "Patriotism is supporting your country all the time, and your government when it deserves it." We may hope that our leaders and our government stand up for our ideals, and there are many times in our history when that's occurred. But when our laws, our leaders, or our government are out of alignment with our ideals, then the dissent of ordinary Americans may prove to be one of the truest expressions of patriotism.

> —*Senator Barack Obama, "The America We Love,"*
> *June 30, 2008, Independence, MO*

THE CHALLENGE

To show you how to stage a media event, here's a description of what we did during the last election to expose the real John McCain.

Whenever you hold a press event, you want to focus on one simple message. In our case, it was this: Senator John McCain would largely bring four more years of George W. Bush for our country. So we brainstormed imagery that would embody the McCain = Bush idea.

We thought of a getting a live parrot, to show that McCain "parrots" Bush, but we worried that we'd have PETA activists all over us. We thought of a rubber stamp, illustrating that McCain would rubber-stamp Bush policies, but we thought it would be a too static. We thought of a "hug mobile," a flatbed trailer carrying Bush and McCain in a permanent embrace, but there was no time. (We ran a hug-mobile tour later.)

In the end, we decided that because Bush and McCain are "two peas in a pod," we'd buy a pea-pod costume on the Internet, and replace the peas with photos of Bush and McCain—a perfect on-message prop for a media event.

The next step was to unveil the prop at a time when reporters would be looking for an oppositional story about McCain. This was easy, because McCain was visiting our hometown. We'd find a volunteer to dress in the costume and be there early, to catch journalists coming inside.

We drafted a news advisory to let reporters know we'd be there, on the sidewalk in front, where you don't need a permit as long as you leave a path for pedestrians to pass. Of course, we had a media list in place, but if you don't have one, call up a group that supports what you're doing and ask for its list. Or find one online. We sent the news advisory out by e-mail, and we called the key journalists to make sure they got it. That's important. Journalists are overwhelmed with news releases. You need to call to confirm that they get yours.

After writing some pea-pod talking points, with facts and citations showing why Bush and McCain are the same, and conducting a practice question-and-answer session, we were ready.

We mobilized a group of supporters to stand with us and our pea pod. That evening we were featured on two local TV newscasts, and a day later we were on national news. We understand it's a tall order to organize a press conference or rally, but there's another option: Just show up.

PRACTICAL INFORMATION

- Journalists at large media outlets receive scores of news releases or more each week. But they also say that they are receiving fewer phone calls in recent years, as people rely exclusively on e-mail.

- Fewer than 5 percent of Americans take part in a protest or demonstration annually.

- People with more leisure time on their hands are not more likely to volunteer for events than those with less free time.

- Schedule a press conference during lunch or on a weekend if you are looking to have others join you.

(Sources: Pew Research Center for People and the Press, Corporation for National and Community Service)

WHAT *YOU* CAN DO

FOR STAGING YOUR OWN MEDIA EVENT . . .

Practice a news conference in advance. Have everyone involved read their statements and answer a couple questions.

Try to have a visual element, like our pea pod, with every news conference. Television news wants more than just talking heads. Think infotainment.

Don't run a news conference for longer than 15 minutes, and have no more than four speakers.

Send your news release to a specific reporter at a newspaper, and call him or her as a follow-up. Don't just send it to the "news department." At a local TV station, ask for the "assignment editor."

At your press event, distribute no more than five pages of background material, including a one-page news release containing the properly spelled names and titles of each speaker.

Don't give up. Sometimes not a single reporter will attend your news event. On any day, you never know what your competition is.

Here's the advisory we sent by e-mail about our event described at the beginning of this chapter.

GIANT PEA POD TO MEET MCCAIN:
Bush and McCain are "Peas in a Pod"
For Immediate Release

Contact: Michael Huttner, ProgressNow Action, 303-991-1900

What: Giant Pea Pod and others to hold press conference and attend Senator John McCain's Denver Town Hall. They will also hand out pea pods to show McCain's economic policies are just like Bush's.

When: Monday, July 7, press conference at 9:30am, immediately before McCain's speech.

Where: In front of the Denver Center for the Performing Arts, on 14th between Curtis and Champa.

Why: The pea pod event is designed to emphasize that Senator McCain and President George Bush are "two peas in a pod" as their policies are nearly identical on the economy and other key issues confronting America.

"Bush and McCain are obviously two peas in a pod when it comes to messing up our economy," said Michael Huttner, Executive Director of ProgressNow Action, Colorado's largest online progressive advocacy organization. "No matter how many green beans you eat, Bush and McCain's economic policies are bad for America."

The eight-foot pea pod costume features Bush and McCain as peas.

McCain will be giving a speech on economic issues at the DCPA Monday. The press conference is at 9:30am as doors open at 10am.

(To see TV news clips of this event, search on YouTube.com for "Bush McCain Pea Pod" and "Carol Kreck.")

FOR ATTENDING A RALLY OR PROTEST...

Set a goal to attend at least one public event every other month where you'd expect to find reporters. It's important to maintain the visibility for Obama, and sometimes we forget to get out of the living room.

Make a handmade sign. Even if you've got only 10 minutes to scratch something down on cardboard, do it. Authentic expression is influential.

Get there early. News personnel will sometimes get to a rally early and leave early.

Don't argue with counter-protesters. If far-right-wingers show up, don't argue with them. Conflict distracts the news media and others from the purpose of the rally.

Chant! This adds energy and strength to a rally, even if it's small.

Have fun. There's an unfortunate perception that rallies are drudgery. They're not. You see people you know. You see crazy stuff, like people in costumes. You hear chants. It's up to us to make rallies good entertainment, and they usually are.

RECOMMENDED RESOURCES

Effect Communications, www.effectcommunications.com, is Jason's Web site. It has free step-by-step guides on organizing your own media event. You can also buy his book, *Making the News: A Guide for Activists and Nonprofits* (NY: Basic Books, 2003).

Congress.org, www.congress.org, allows you to search for individual reporters or media organizations at the local and national level. (Look in "Media Guide.")

PollingReport.com, www.pollingreport.com, posts free polling information, aggregated by issue.

Polltrack.com, www.polltrack.com, is a comprehensive, up-to-the-minute picture of what voters are thinking and feeling.

Protest.net, www.protest.net, is an international listing of protests and information about them.

[36]

Hold Extremists Accountable

> We must form grassroot structures that would hold me and other
> elected officials more accountable for their actions. The right wing, the
> Christian right, has a done a good job of building these organizations of
> accountability, much better than the left or progressive forces have.
>
> —*State Senate Candidate Barack Obama,*
> *"What Makes Obama Run,"*
> Chicago Reader, *December 8, 1995*

THE CHALLENGE

You should have seen the rally we attended the day that President Obama
signed the economic stimulus package. The extreme right-wingers were
trying to convince people that President Obama's new law was filled
with "pork-barrel" spending that would benefit special interests. Their
rally featured a live pig, literally snorting around the podium, and a
roasted pig, with its head still on, displayed in front of the small crowd
and a throng of TV cameras and journalists with notepads.

These extremists were in hog heaven. They didn't care that President
Obama's bill was designed to save or create 3.5 million jobs by funding
roads, schools, high-speed rails, home weatherization, and more things
that America desperately needs. But since when does the extreme right
wing care about the facts when they go on the attack? That's why we
need to hold them accountable.

So we wandered through the crowd with a giant sign showing how the unemployment rate spiked last year, and we challenged the conservative speakers' credibility on economic issues, given that former President George W. Bush had just finished presiding over the destruction of the global economy. We waved our sign near the ultra-right syndicated columnist Michelle Malkin, who was a featured speaker, as she carved the roast pig and handed sandwiches to swarming righties. But more importantly, we introduced ourselves to reporters and told them we were there to present the other side. Our quotes were included in TV and newspaper accounts of the rally.

During the entire rally, a man with a swastika sign in his hands stood on the stage, and not one conservative bothered to ask him to put away his sign or, God forbid, get off the stage. This guy wasn't just out there on the fringes of the rally. He was on the stage next to the speakers in front.

So our colleague got a photo of the "swastika guy" up there, and later, another one of him hugging columnist Malkin. We supplied these photos to blogs and reporters, and the next day our photo of Malkin hugging the swastika guy was on tens of thousands of Web sites across the country.

That's what we mean by holding right-wingers accountable: confronting them and exposing them in the media.

PRACTICAL INFORMATION

- One of the reasons to hold the extreme right wing accountable is to weaken the influence of the far-right "echo chamber." It's a loose network of commentators and media outlets, including blogs, radio, and television stations, some supported by the same far-right-wing foundations. These outlets tend to glom on to a news item or allegation and offer the same far-right-wing interpretation or outright lie about it. Or the echo chamber may "report" on a news item that's bogus or highly dubious. Their unified focus can push a hyped or false allegation or news story into the wider public debate, and sometimes generate attention from credible news sources.

- On stations owned by the top five commercial radio corporations, 91 percent of talk radio programming is conservative, compared with 9 percent progressive.

- Thirty-six percent of registered voters self-identify as Democrats, versus 26 percent as Republicans. Of the 37 percent who say they are independent, 15 percent lean Democratic, 10 percent Republican, and 12 percent have no preference.

(Sources: SourceWatch.org, Center for American Progress, Pew Center for People and the Press)

WHAT *YOU* CAN DO

Track the far right. To find out what the extreme right wing is up to so you can respond to them, subscribe to far-right-wing newsletters and blogs in your community. They'll spread the word about protests and tactics extremists are using to attack Obama. (For far-right-wing Web sites to track, see resources in "Reach Out to Conservatives," as well as at the end of this chapter.)

Select a way to hold the far right accountable. In addition to attending their protests, as described above, consider these options: writing letters to the editor or guest commentaries (op-eds) for your local newspaper, going to lectures by arch conservatives, calling talk radio shows, or commenting on extreme-right-wing blogs.

Think visually. If you plan to protest at a far-right-wing event, make a really big sign or banner. Be funny, if you can, and don't be shy about approaching any media in attendance.

Get there early. The news media like to arrive at rallies well before they start. If you get there early to counter-protest, you'll have a better chance of scoring coverage.

Practice your lines. Get your facts straight and practice your 12-second statement before you counter-protest. A few minutes of practice can make all the difference in delivering an effective sound bite.

Don't delay. When extreme right-wingers start spreading lies, confront them immediately. You lose your media appeal and momentum by delaying.

Don't rely on others. Lots of us have good intentions to take action, but the truth is that most of us don't get it done. Reach out to others, but make sure it gets done yourself.

RECOMMENDED RESOURCES

Americans for Prosperity, www.americansforprosperity.org, is a conservative pro-business coalition. Find links to other far-right-wing organizations on this Web site. Track what the extreme right does by signing up for e-mail alerts.

Citizens for Responsibility and Ethics in Washington, www.citizensforethics .org, is a top-notch DC operation that uses legal procedures to hold elected officials accountable. They are always open to tips concerning federal lawmakers.

Communications Consortium Media Center, www.ccmc.org, provides a list of editors of the op-ed pages for major newspapers, and is a good place to find information on submitting op-eds.

ProgressNow, www.progressnow.org, is a state-based online network of organizations that holds the right wing accountable. Sign up for their alerts and contact them with any tips.

50 Simple Things You Can Do to Fight the Right, (Berkeley, CA: Earthworks Press, 2006) a book by Earthworks Action Network, provides a number of creative and useful items to help hold the far right accountable.

The Republican Noise Machine: Right-Wing Media and How It Corrupts Democracy (NY: Random House, 2004), a book by David Brock, provides an excellent description of the extreme right wing.

SourceWatch, www.sourcewatch.org, is a wiki directory of people and organizations in the news, highlighting far-right-wing media "sources" and the organizations backing them.

VoteSmart, www.votesmart.org, provides information on federal and state lawmakers' voting records and their public statements.

[37]

Feed a Story to a Columnist or Blogger

I think the danger of blogs is that we are only talking to ourselves and people who agree with us. That means that over time we are just reinforcing our own preconceptions and we are not opening up to other ideas and other points of view. One of the things I am always trying to figure out is how to get different bloggers and different points of view communicating so it is a conversation and dialogue, not just all of us cheering each other on.

—Senator Barack Obama,
Heightsmom.blogspot.com, June 4, 2006

THE CHALLENGE

Most bloggers don't go out and report the news. They don't usually cover a meeting at city hall. They use the news of the day as a springboard for comment and analysis. It's the same with newspaper columnists. But they present their views in about 650 printed words, while bloggers can go on forever.

Both need stuff to opine about. And that's where you come in.

You can e-mail information and story ideas to both columnists and bloggers. Most of them are looking for local angles on the big stories of the day. Bloggers are more interested in analyzing the politics or facts of an issue, with a combative and entertaining edge. Newspaper columnists, on the other hand, usually want a good story about local citizens, and they're more balanced.

So this means if you're doing something innovative and fun to promote President Obama's agenda, let a columnist know about it. And explain it with a story line, not a recitation of facts. If you're just trying to spread the word about false or manipulated facts that are spinning through the news unchallenged—and you want to get it out there fast—let a blogger know about it.

PRACTICAL INFORMATION

- The word "blog" was formed by combining "web" and "log." Blogs were originally personal diaries, updated frequently. Now most popular blogs are updated throughout the day with fresh material.

- There are over 20 million bloggers in America, with over 1.5 million making some money from it, according to the *Wall Street Journal.*

- You rarely find a blog that doesn't allow you to post comments directly. So it can be easier to simply respond to a blog post than to lobby the blogger to include your information. However, it can pay to feed bloggers information for them to use, because your idea or facts can be more credible and entertaining if they come from a blogger directly.

- Many newspaper columnists also have a blog—and the information they want for their blogs can be very different than what they use for columns.

WHAT *YOU* CAN DO

To reach a columnist, first try e-mail. You'll usually get a response. If not, call a few times before leaving a voice-mail message because personal conversations are more persuasive. (But practice your "pitch" before you call.)

You'll find contact information for most columnists at the end of their columns. Or you can find this information online—or call the newspaper.

For bloggers, e-mail is often the only option, and blogger contact info is usually available on the site.

Don't irritate bloggers or columnists by sending them information they care nothing about. Read their blogs and columns first, and then send them material that matches their interests and styles.

If you're trying to communicate information to a targeted group, such as youth voters, identify blogs that reach your target audience.

Find blogs by looking at the "blogroll" of blogs you like. The blogroll is a list of blogs that often appears on the left- or right-hand side of a blog's home page. It's the blogger's favorite blogs.

Some blogs allow you to set up your own "diary" or blog within the site. On these blogs, the lead blogger-in-chief will select some diary entries and display them more prominently.

RECOMMENDED RESOURCES

Congress.org, www.congress.org, lists columnist contacts in its "Media Guide."

Daily Kos, www.dailykos.com, is the leading progressive blog in America, founded by Markos Moulitsas Zúniga. His book *Crashing the Gate: Netroots, Grassroots and the Rise of People-Powered Politics* (White River Junction, VT: Chelsea Green, 2006) provides firsthand history of the rise of progressive political blogs.

Instapundit.com, www.drudgereport.com, lets you learn what the extreme-right-wing blogosphere is up to.

Lefty Bogs, www.leftyblogs.com, is a good list of blogs.

Slate, www.slate.com/id/2207061, has the article "How to Blog: Advice from Arianna Huffington, Om Malik, and More of the Web's Best Pundits," December 18, 2008.

[38]

Support Obama in a Letter to the Editor or Online Comment

I made the same argument in a letter I sent to the left-leaning blog Daily Kos in September 2005, after a number of advocacy groups and activists had attacked some of my Democratic colleagues for voting to confirm Chief Justice John Roberts. My staff was a little nervous about the idea; since I had voted against Roberts's confirmation, they saw no reason for me to agitate such a vocal part of the Democratic base. But I had come to appreciate the give-and-take that the blogs afforded, and in the days following the posting of my letter, in true democratic fashion, more than six hundred people posted their comments.

—*Senator Barack Obama,*
"Republicans and Democrats," The Audacity of Hope

THE CHALLENGE

After President Obama's economic stimulus bill had cleared Congress and was signed into law, the battle to win over public opinion was just beginning. In the coming weeks President Obama traveled thousands of miles, held his first prime-time news conference, and led a major communications offensive to explain what his stimulus spending would do and why it was so important.

As an ordinary Obama admirer, you may find moments like these frustrating as hell because, as the PR war heats up and Obama gets attacked, you want to do something. But what?

For immediate gratification and for the good of the country, you can respond to media coverage with quick and focused commentary. This can be effective, especially if many of us act together.

In the case of the stimulus legislation, journalists descended from around the country to cover not only the signing of the bill into law, but the subsequent events staged by President Obama to support it. Reacting to the news of an event like this gives you the chance to be a mini–echo chamber and promote President Obama's agenda.

PRACTICAL INFORMATION

- Letter to the editor. Newspaper editors will tell you that the pages devoted to these letters are among the most widely read sections of the newspaper, and newspapers—despite circulation declines—are still a major news sources in America. And even if your letter doesn't appear in the print edition, many newspapers upload all their letters to the editor to their Web sites. So a letter to the editor is worth the effort.

- Online comments. Most online editions of newspapers allow readers to post comments in response to news stories. Many local TV stations and other news outlets also allow for comments by people like us. Your comments in support of Obama can make a difference. In fact, it's clear that many more people read the comments boards online than post comments there. And unfortunately, it's frequently conservative comments that dominate. All the more reason to post your own.

- During the 2008 election, one in five of the people who used the Internet posted political commentary online, according to the Pew Internet and American Life Project.

WHAT *YOU* CAN DO

Keep comments under 200 words. There are two reasons for this. First, newspaper editors seldom publish anything over 200 words, and second, more people read the shorter letters than the longer ones. Be sure to include your phone number as they may want to call to get your OK before they publish.

Make same-day responses. Editors at major newspapers like to publish letters about today's news in tomorrow's newspaper. So if you wait a day, your chances of success seriously diminish. And of course, the sooner you post an online comment, the more people will read it as they go online to read the day's news. Wait a few days, and the online audience has sailed away to fresher news.

Respond to specific stories. With letters to the editor, reference the specific news article that you're writing about. And make sure to include your name, e-mail address, street address, and phone number, so editors can quickly contact you for confirmation.

Comment on blogs. Local and national blogs are becoming the front lines in public opinion formation. Post your opinions on local and national blogs, too.

RECOMMENDED RESOURCES

Fenton Communications, www.fenton.com/resources/industry-guides, offers guides on effective communications for nonprofits and advocacy groups.

Green Media Toolshed, www.greenmediatoolshed.org, has information about online communications for advocacy groups.

Nancy Schwartz and Company, www.nancyschwartz.com/letters_to_
the_editor.html, gives advice on how to write effective letters to
the editor.

The Spin Project, www.spinproject.org, gives tips on how to write letters
to the editor and other advice on grassroots media.

[39]

Reach Out to Conservatives

A few days after I won the Democratic nomination, I received an e-mail from a doctor who told me that while he voted for me in the primary, he had a serious concern that might prevent him from voting for me in the general election. He described himself as a Christian who was strongly pro-life, but that's not what was preventing him from voting for me.

What bothered the doctor was an entry that my campaign staff had posted on my Web site—an entry that said I would fight "right-wing ideologues who want to take away a woman's right to choose." The doctor said that he had assumed I was a reasonable person, but that if I truly believed that every pro-life individual was simply an ideologue who wanted to inflict suffering on women, then I was not very reasonable. He wrote, "I do not ask at this point that you oppose abortion, only that you speak about this issue in fair-minded words."

Fair-minded words.

After I read the doctor's letter, I wrote back to him and thanked him. I didn't change my position, but I did tell my staff to change the words on my Web site. And I said a prayer that night that I might extend the same presumption of good faith to others that the doctor had extended to me. Because when we do that—when we open our hearts and our minds to those who may not think like we do or believe what we do—that's when we discover at least the possibility of common ground.

> *President Barack Obama,*
> *Notre Dame graduation speech,*
> *May 17, 2009, South Bend, IN*

THE CHALLENGE

As a legislator, Barack Obama won bipartisan support for legislation that reformed welfare and stopped racial profiling. Luckily, we don't have to join with our conservative neighbors or friends to pass legislation, but we should engage them in conversation about the issues. That's in line with President Obama's eloquent plea to at least listen to opposing views and treat those who hold them with respect.

We're not advocating a "Kumbaya" approach to politics, because our differences with the right wing are too fundamental. But most conservatives aren't on the high-profile extreme-right-wing edge of the Republican Party. Most just think their values are more in line with Republicans.

In reality, as poll after poll shows, most Americans, regardless of their political affiliation, are much closer to progressives, when you scratch the surface, than they are to conservatives—on issues ranging from health care and education to trade and the environment.

So our challenge is to convince more conservatives that Obama's policies reflect their beliefs more than those of so-called conservatives.

PRACTICAL INFORMATION

- Eighty-five percent of likely voters, including left- and right-leaning ones, think that "big companies" and "political action committees" have too much influence on politics.

- About half of U.S. adults think the two-party system has "real problems."

- Most Americans are religiously tolerant. A clear majority of most religious traditions believe that their own religion does not provide the only path to salvation.

- Among those who use the Internet for obtaining political information or for other political purposes, 44 percent of Democrats and 35 percent of Republicans mostly visit Web sites that share their own political views.

(Sources: Harris Poll, NBC News/Wall Street Journal Poll, Pew Internet and American Life Project)

WHAT *YOU* CAN DO

First, connect with conservatives on a personal level. Don't rush into political discussion with a conservative. Try to connect over some shared life experience, like your upbringing or parenting, and then move to political issues. One way is to begin the conversation with "So what do you love to do?" or "What do you care about most?"

Focus on one conservative. Jason's wife decided to focus her energy on converting one conservative she knows quite well—her mother. She strategically recruited her siblings, especially her brother, to reinforce the messages she was sending her mom in conversations and e-mails. It worked. Guess who she voted for.

Talk about values. Whenever we try to have a serious conversation with conservatives, we fall back on our belief that the core principles of conservatives are actually better reflected in progressive values and policies. For example, conservatives say they're for "opportunity," but it's really progressives who promote the kind of red-blooded opportunity that's valued by many self-identified conservatives. The left-leaning Opportunity Agenda notes in an excellent report: "Crucial to the promise of opportunity is that all people have access to a good education, a decent job at a living wage, an affordable place to live, and high-quality health care." So you can see how "opportunity" provides common ground for progressives to connect with conservatives. It's not hard, in a conversation, to identify a value, such as equal opportunity, responsibility, or independence, that conservatives identify in themselves. We need to show conservatives that progressives are better stewards of basic American values.

Act like Obama. He's a great role model for communicating progressive values. He's competent, confident, reasonable, tolerant, and respectful—just to mention a few qualities that we could all benefit from having. And he's cool.

Be civil. No matter what they say. Don't level personal attacks.

Keep it simple. In conversations and interviews, stick to a single point or two that you want your conservative to carry away.

Lower expectations. Obama can't solve all our problems, but who could be doing better? Even if you don't like him, doesn't Obama deserve a chance after eight years of Bush? A friend was recently asked by a man itching to score some debate points, "So what do you think of Obama now?" "Compared to what?" my friend replied with a smile, "President Bush?" Then they had a perfectly civil conversation about the Treasury Department under Obama versus Bush.

Look at listening as a strength. Listen to conservatives whenever possible. Listen to the media. Know what they're saying so you understand your audience.

Be confident and concise, yet inquisitive. It's a conversation, a give-and-take. You don't need to have all the answers.

RECOMMENDED RESOURCES

Campaign for Liberty, www.campaignforliberty.com, is a far-right-wing organization. Keep abreast of far-right-wing activities and learn about how right-wingers think by monitoring this and similar sites. Other far-right-wing sites include: www.freedomworks.org, www.resistnet .com, www.frc.org, www.conservative.org, and the Republican National Committee's official group on www.facebook.com.

Frameworks Institute, www.frameworksinstitute.org, aims to apply scholarly research on framing and communications to the nonprofit sector.

George Lakoff, is the author of the bestselling *Don't Think of an Elephant!: Know Your Values and Frame the Debate—The Essential Guide for Progressives* (White River Junction, VT: Chelsea Green, 2004).

Opportunity Agenda, www.opportunityagenda.org, promotes the expansion of opportunity in America, with attention to communications.

How to Win Friends and Influence People (NY: Simon & Schuster, 1936), the classic book by Dale Carnegie, teaches you how to bond with anyone, including those you disagree with politically.

Talk to Action, www.talk2action.org, will help you understand and counter the Christian right.

Transpartisan Alliance, http://network.transpartisan.net, is an informal network whose mission is to put partisan politics aside to obtain practical, important solutions to our country's needs.

Utne Reader, www.utne.com/2007-11-01/politics/the-great-divide.aspx, gives tips on talking through disagreements.

Harness the New Media

There was another lesson to be learned: As soon as Ms. Noonan's column hit, it went racing across the Internet, appearing on every far-right-wing Web site as proof of what an arrogant, shallow boob I was (just the quote Ms. Noonan selected, and not the essay itself, generally made an appearance on these sites). In that sense, the episode hinted at a more subtle and corrosive aspect of modern media—how a particular narrative, repeated over and over again and hurled through cyberspace at the speed of light, eventually becomes a hard particle of reality; how political caricatures and nuggets of conventional wisdom lodge themselves in our brain without us ever taking the time to examine them.

—*Senator Barack Obama,*
"Politics," The Audacity of Hope

[40]

Use Your Cell Phone
and Text Messages for Change

I've chosen Joe Biden to be my running mate. Joe and I will appear for the first time as running mates this afternoon in Springfield, Illinois—the same place this campaign began more than 19 months ago. I'm excited about hitting the campaign trail with Joe, but the two of us can't do this alone. We need your help to keep building this movement for change.

—*Senator Barack Obama,*
text message, 3:00 a.m. EST, August 23, 2008

THE CHALLENGE

Obama broke the news of his running-mate choice to over a million people via a text message sent to cell phones worldwide. All of you who don't text—or weren't sitting next to someone who does—had to wait.

Okay, maybe you only had to wait five minutes until you heard it on TV, but that wasn't the point of Obama's big text-message announcement. The purpose was to gather cell phone numbers of his supporters. In the months prior, Obama reminded his supporters that he'd reveal his VP choice via text message to anyone who sent a text message to "Obama" (62262) requesting it.

During this time, Obama's cell-phone list doubled a few times to over 1 million, according to Evan Thomas in *A Long Time Coming*. And the list was later used to get people to the polls.

PRACTICAL INFORMATION

- This chapter focuses on text messaging, but the cell phone has many other applications for campaigns and organizing. Learn about these by checking out links in our resources section.

- There are 262 million mobile phones in America, and over 80 percent of us have them. There are over 3 billion mobile phones worldwide, representing a huge opportunity for organizing.

- Half of Americans who have cell phones are text messaging, and the percentage is growing.

- Eighteen- to 25-year-olds send an average of 2,500 text messages per month.

(Sources: CTIA, MobileActive.org)

FROM THE FRONT LINES

For the campaign, we hoped you'd subscribe to Barack Obama's text list because we knew those messages were being opened, getting read and making an impact. There was an extremely high rate of return from mobile communication at lightning speed. Think about it, the cell phone is the device that's with people almost 24 hours a day—not their computer.

—Scott Goodstein, external online director, Barack Obama Campaign, and founder of Revolution Messaging

WHAT *YOU* CAN DO

Think about your goal and audience. Does your campaign goal require speed and substantial involvement by young people, who are still the major users of text messaging?

Weigh your options. It can be expensive and time-consuming to set up a text-messaging operation—in part because it's not easy to get people's cell phone numbers. That's one reason there's so much less spam in the text-message world, compared to e-mail.

Select a short code and register it. This is the five- or six-digit number that people use to get on your text message list. Obama's code was 62262, which spelled out "Obama" on the phone keys. So, by texting the number 62262, anyone could request text messages from the Obama Campaign. Consulting companies will register your short code with cellular providers (like Verizon, T-Mobile, AT&T, etc.) and set you up with the ability to send bulk text messages and to manage your database of cell phone numbers.

How will you get cell phone numbers? Obama had a great draw to harvest cell phone numbers—himself. But how will you do it? If you're going to plan a campaign using text messaging, make sure you have a plan to get cell phone numbers. One way that's been effective with people who use cell phones the most is to offer premiums—small gifts—for signing up.

When people respond to your short code, send a text message thanking them and asking for geographical information. That way, you can involve people in actual campaigns on the ground because you will know where they live. A street address is best, plus an e-mail, but a zip code is essential. Don't ask for too much further information too quickly, because text messaging is almost always brief.

Even if you're not texting now, follow the technology and collect cell phone numbers for future use. Cell phone technology is advancing quickly and the ways that phones can be used in campaigns—particularly as more smart phones do more of the things computers can do—is growing. Whether you decide to use text messaging or not, you should start collecting cell phone numbers now as part of the regular contact information that you gather at meetings, registrations, etc. You might want the cell phone numbers down the line.

RECOMMENDED RESOURCES

CREDO Mobile, www.workingassetts.com, is a cell phone service that mobilizes its customers to support progressive causes.

Mobile Active, www.mobileactive.org, has resources for activists using cell phones worldwide.

Mobile Commons, www.mcommons.com, is a firm specializing in applying cell phone technology to the needs of activist organizations and businesses. See case studies on the use of phones in campaigns on their Web site.

Revolution Messaging, www.revolutionmessaging.com, is a firm that specializes in social networking and mobile messaging.

Twitter, www.twitter.com, is a free social-messaging utility for staying connected in real time via your computer or cell phone.

Be a Media Watchdog
and Challenge Journalists

To make the deadline, to maintain the market share and feed the cable news beast, reporters start to move in packs, working off the same news releases, the same set pieces, the same stock figures. Meanwhile, for busy and therefore casual news consumers, a well-worn narrative is not entirely unwelcome. It makes few demands on our thought or time; it's quick and easy to digest. Accepting spin is easier on everybody.

—*Senator Barack Obama,*
"Politics," The Audacity of Hope

THE CHALLENGE

More than any other president, Barack Obama is trying to communicate directly with us via the White House's Web site. He's continuing to use blogs, Facebook, Twitter, YouTube, and more to bypass journalists who can cut his message short or distort it.

But the traditional news media are still the number one source of political information for most Americans. And depending on the media outlet that's delivering the information, this is a good thing. Reporters and editors hold public officials accountable, and investigate unethical behavior.

But even the best journalists need to watchdog themselves. And the worst of the so-called journalists out there should be held accountable on a daily basis, as a spin through most talk radio or cable TV shows demonstrates. Many of Obama's initiatives, no matter how methodically planned and rolled out, will be unfairly characterized in the mainstream media. It doesn't mean reporters are biased necessarily, though some are definitely biased. It just comes with the territory.

You can help Obama by fighting for better journalism and accountability from reporters.

FROM THE FRONT LINES

The stakes have never been higher. Holding the media accountable for what they report is more important than ever. Regardless of the issue you are most passionate about—health care reform, economic recovery, solving the climate crisis, etc.—the media dictate the terms of our public debate. Sitting on the sidelines in this fight for accountability just isn't an option if you really want to see progress in the years to come."

—*David Brock, founder and CEO of Media Matters for America*

PRACTICAL INFORMATION

- Community activists need to work with reporters to get their messages out and get covered in the news. Criticizing journalists too much can obviously strain the relationship between an activist and a reporter. Some activists refrain from criticizing journalists, leaving this role to others.

- There are a total of 355 journalists working at the state capitols across the country. That's 32 percent less than six years ago. In the past two and a half years, 30,000 journalists have lost their jobs.

- Some larger media outlets, such as the *New York Times*, the *Washington Post*, and National Public Radio, have a staff position called the "ombudsman," "reader representative," or the like. This person's job is to respond to your concerns about coverage.

(Sources: American Journalism Review, journalismjobs.com)

WHAT *YOU* CAN DO

Be specific. The best media watchdogs document their criticisms of the news media, pointing to specific instances of bias or inaccuracy. Once you do this, you should ask a journalist for a meeting to discuss your criticism. Focus on local news. Local outlets will be less interested in hearing criticism of stories that they run from the Associated Press or the *New York Times*. They'll be more open to discussing problems in coverage they produce themselves.

If you spot an error, complain to journalists directly by e-mail or phone. Don't go to their editor unless you are ignored.

If you think of a good local story about Obama that hasn't been covered, call media outlets and pitch it. Try to identify a specific reporter who covers the type of story you're thinking of.

Target talk radio. Local talk radio around the country is dominated by the right wing. And sometimes the falsehoods and bigotry spewed there about Obama are heard only by die-hard far-right-wingers. You can expose this nastiness by documenting it, sharing it with allies, and staging protests demanding accountability from talk show hosts and their advertisers.

Be aware of the difficulties faced by serious journalists today as you complain about coverage. Mainstream journalism is in serious decline. Advertising revenue is flowing away from large newspaper, radio, and TV outlets and moving toward more targeted vehicles, mostly on the Web. This has resulted in the layoffs of journalists across the country, particularly at newspapers.

Become a member of a media-activism group. National groups like Fairness and Accuracy in Reporting (FAIR) and Media Matters for America regularly suggest ways for citizens to pressure media outlets, often at the national level.

RECOMMENDED RESOURCES

Fairness and Accuracy in Reporting (FAIR), www.fair.org, is a media watchdog group whose Web site has how-to information for activists.

Media Matters for America, www.mediamatters.org, reports on extreme right-wing misinformation in the media.

PR Watch, www.prwatch.org, focuses on media manipulation by the PR industry, brought to you by the Center for Media and Democracy.

News Hounds, www.newshounds.us, exposes lies on the FOX Network.

[42]

Make a YouTube Video

After nearly a year on the campaign trail, I've seen a lot of things that have touched me deeply, but I had to share this with you. Sharing this video, which was created by supporters, is one more way to help start a conversation with your friends, family, co-workers, and anyone else who will be voting soon about the issues important to them in this election.

—Michelle Obama, in a mass e-mail
forwarding will.i.am's "Yes We Can"
YouTube video, February 4, 2008

THE CHALLENGE

Here's another story about someone who wanted to do more for Obama, and found a way to get it done.

Will.i.am is a musician with the rap group Black Eyed Peas. He heard Obama give a speech, and he was so inspired that he recruited dozens of his artist friends and spent three days putting the speech to music. He uploaded it on YouTube, and soon millions and millions of people were watching it, around the world. (Assuming you've already seen it, check it out again. It's great.)

Will.i.am didn't ask the Obama campaign for permission to make the video. He just did it. It didn't hurt that will.i.am is a celebrity and he recruited fellow celebs to be in his video. But, still, the video exemplifies how something can take off on YouTube.

Jesse Dylan, Bob Dylan's son, who helped produce the video, told the *Boston Globe*, "We didn't even have any giant aspirations. We wanted to do something for Obama, but this has taken off beyond our wildest expectations."

PRACTICAL INFORMATION

- Seventy-two percent of 18- to 29-year-olds and 65 percent of 30- to 49-year-olds used the Internet for political purposes during the 2008 election campaign. Among these Internet users, 67 percent of the younger group and 62 percent of the older group watched online political videos.

- During the 2008 campaign, 21 percent of Obama's supporters shared videos, photos, or audio content with others, versus 16 percent of McCain supporters.

- Video-editing software is standard on many computers, and it's easy to use. Many people don't even realize they have it on their computers.

(Source: Pew Internet and American Life Project)

WHAT *YOU* CAN DO

Think about your goal. Do you want to help Obama get legislation through Congress? Do you want to inspire supporters?

Refine your message and target an audience. Make sure the core message to advance your goal is captured in your video— and that it will appeal to the folks you want to see it.

Select appropriate imagery. Find spokespeople and imagery that won't turn off the people you're trying to reach.

Keep it short. You'll have the most success if you keep it to below two minutes, like a TV ad.

Be creative. will.i.am decided to sing a speech. What's next?

Connect your video to President Obama's agenda. Visit the Web site of Organizing for America to get ideas.

If you've got an idea but can't do it yourself, find someone who can. Your idea may be just what someone else wants to do.

You don't have to be a pro. The strength of many YouTube videos comes from their authenticity, the fact that they aren't polished pieces of propaganda. So this frees you to try almost anything, as long as you keep it short. If you've uploaded a YouTube video, you know how easy it is. You just log on to YouTube.com and follow the simple instructions. So there's no need to be scared if you've never done it, as long as you have the ability to shoot a short digital video.

An example of a common person who made a huge hit was Phil De Vellis. He made "Vote Different," a take-off on a 1984 Super Bowl ad by Apple, without the involvement of the Obama Campaign. "I made the ad on a Sunday afternoon in my apartment using my personal equipment (a Mac and some software), uploaded it to YouTube, and sent links around to blogs. This ad was not the first citizen ad, and it will not be the last. The game has changed."

It's not hard to edit video, but don't feel obligated to do so. Simplify things by shooting a video that's short and requires no editing.

RECOMMENDED RESOURCES

Brave New Foundation. www.bravenewfoundation.org/index.php, works with campaigns and organizers on new media projects, including videos.

"Yes We Can" is will.i.am's YouTube song/video that raced across the Internet. Go to www.youtube.com and type "will.i.am yes we can" in the search box.

YouTube, www.youtube.com, itself is a great resource because the best way to figure out what makes a successful YouTube video is to spend some time perusing YouTube.

[43]

Pass on Online Action Alerts

When I look at what happened in my race, the ability of the Internet to spread the word about a campaign for a candidate who wasn't that well known was absolutely critical.

—Senator Barack Obama,
Ohio Democratic State Dinner, June 4, 2006

THE CHALLENGE

Despite all the new things to do online, one of the first and most basic Internet activities is still the most powerful when it comes to politics: the simple act of forwarding an e-mail to people you know. Pollsters and common sense say that information received from a personal source, someone personally known to the recipient, has the most power to persuade. So e-mails sent from person to person can be hugely influential.

You can create YouTube videos and Facebook groups. You can download mail-in ballot request forms or find out where to vote. You can find voting records.

But forwarding information and infotainment is still key. Just ask Republican Senator George Allen, whose "macaca moment," posted on YouTube, killed his re-election bid in 2006. And ask Senator John McCain.

PRACTICAL INFORMATION

- During the 2008 election campaign, 59 percent of Internet users shared political information using e-mail, instant messaging, or text messaging. So most Internet users will pass on campaign facts, entertainment, or other political content via the web.

- Thirty-eight percent of Internet users communicated with others about politics during the 2008 election campaign. This means discussing the issues involved, perhaps in response to a forwarded e-mail.

- Relatively few Americans (15 percent) rely on the Internet for election news. But this is still more than twice what it was in 2004 (6 percent).

(Sources: Pew Internet and American Life Project, Pew Research Center for People and the Press.)

WHAT *YOU* CAN DO

Forward e-mails explaining what people can do. Make an extra effort to forward e-mails that point to a specific action. The e-mails we receive now that President Obama is in office—about writing a letter to Congress or attending a rally—aren't as likely to be the kind of funny or angry e-mails that typically get forwarded.

Sign up to receive e-mails. Take a few minutes to make sure you're receiving e-mails from organizations that are tracking President Obama's progress and mobilizing people to support him. If you're not on the President's Organizing for America's e-mail list, sign up now. Locate other organizations in your community or nationally that are tracking President Obama's agenda and mobilizing people to support it.

Segment your e-mail list. We create sub-lists of our larger e-mail lists, so it's easy to forward e-mails to different types of people.

Forward information using social media. Some people don't use e-mail at all anymore, preferring to forward information via social networks like Facebook. If you're one of those people, send action information to your Facebook groups, write about it on your Facebook wall, or Twitter it.

The key is to keep forwarding e-mails, even now when the intensity of the election campaign is behind us. Much of what we have to do now will be less charged, less dramatic for those of us who aren't political junkies. So the game of forwarding e-mails to help President Obama requires that we think strategically about what needs to get done, and forward e-mails that advance our strategic goals, even if we feel less engaged.

RECOMMENDED RESOURCES

Citizen Engagement Laboratory, www.engagementlab.org, focuses on diverse audiences.

MoveOn.org, www.moveon.org, can send you action-oriented e-mails if you sign up.

Organizing for America, www.barackobama.com, is the president's organization. Spread the word about these alerts.

ProgressNow, www.progressnow.org, sends action alerts in selected states. Just sign up to receive them.

TrueMajority.org, www.truemajority.org, believes in social justice, giving children a decent start in life, protecting the environment, and America working in cooperation with the world community. Fill out a form to receive regular e-mails on national progressive issues.

[44]

Social Network for Obama

- **Interests:** Basketball, writing, spending time w/ kids

- **Favorite Music:** Miles Davis, John Coltrane, Bob Dylan, Stevie Wonder, Johann Sebastian Bach (cello suites), and The Fugees

- **Favorite Movies:** Casablanca, The Godfather (I & II), Lawrence of Arabia, and One Flew Over the Cuckoo's Nest

- **Favorite Books:** Song of Solomon (Toni Morrison), Moby Dick, Shakespeare's tragedies, Parting the Waters, Gilead (Robinson), Self-Reliance (Emerson), The Bible, Lincoln's collected writings

- **Favorite TV Shows:** Sportscenter

- **Favorite Quotations:** "The arc of the moral universe is long, but it bends toward justice." (Martin Luther King, Jr.)

—President Barack Obama, from his Facebook page

THE CHALLENGE

Barack Obama's presidential campaign took organizing to a new level. And social networking was a big part of his online success.

Social networks (like Facebook and Twitter) are Web sites where members can share information with other members who agree to do so.

Depending on the social network, they can share photos, video, text, music—pretty much anything digital.

Most social networking is about sharing personal information, like your favorite movie, as President Obama offered on his Facebook page. It's mostly about the personal details of daily life. The most absurd and amusing details are fair game, or actually they're more like the way the social networking game is played.

And it's the personal information that makes social networks a powerful way to communicate about political topics.

Friends have great ability to influence each other. They take each other's opinions seriously. And they're more likely to take political actions suggested by friends. It follows that communicating this type of information digitally to friends is powerful.

So what might this look like in the social networking world? You might send members of your social network a notice about a rally for health care reform, a video of your lunch that was trampled after you dropped it at the rally, and a tweet about other people you saw there, such as your mayor speaking.

PRACTICAL INFORMATION

- Probably the most popular of the social networking sites right now is Facebook.com. Here, you can create your own Facebook page with photos, text, and other digital information. You can send messages to your friends and even add photos and text to their Facebook pages. You can create groups to support political causes.

- Twitter.com allows you to post short messages for your "followers" to receive online. And you can follow the "tweets" of others who allow you to follow them. You can get news on Twitter by following your twittering members of Congress or anyone who's tweeting about something you want to hear about in short bursts of information. A group of people can tag their tweets on a specific topic, and you can request to receive all the tweets using this tag. So you can get lots of little pieces of information on a specific topic.

- Another social network, MySpace.com, is used by younger audiences than Facebook's. It's like a conglomeration of individual Web sites.

- Your social networking won't be as fun or useful if you are all political all the time. Fellow social networkers will begin to tune you out because it's the personal side of social networks that motivates their users. Throw in political information judiciously.

- Obama has 6,068,000 supporters on Facebook, 1,468,000 MySpace friends, 731,000 followers on Twitter, and 169,000 YouTube subscribers.

FROM THE FRONT LINES

For people who aren't part of social networks yet, it's initially weird to be so public with your personal information, but you'll get over it. Sharing the personal information is a big part of the strength of the social network.

—*Jen Caltrider, executive producer of ProgressNow.org*

WHAT *YOU* CAN DO

Join a few social networks. Try Facebook and Twitter first, and see how it goes.

Build your social network. On Facebook, for example, invest at least a few hours getting "friends." That's how you build your network. You do it by requesting that your friends who you find on Facebook be your Facebook friend. It's easy.

Suggest actions and information to your social network. You can tell your friends what actions you're taking for Obama by writing them on your Facebook page or on Twitter. And you can post articles. Your friends can pass this on to their networks. And so it spreads. On Facebook, utilize the status updates.

Comment on other people's posts. You can reinforce or add to a friend's political information by commenting on it or responding to it after they post it.

Join President Obama's social network. Be President Obama's Facebook supporter (www.facebook.com/barackobama), My Space friend (www.myspace.com/barackobama), Twitter follower (http://twitter.com/barackobama), or YouTube subscriber (www .youtube.com/barackobama).

Form a Facebook group in response to breaking news.

Join Facebook groups and invite others to join. The number of people in Facebook groups serves as a social barometer of their legitimacy and power. So, be sure to invite as many people as possible from the get-go and ask them to invite others to join

RECOMMENDED RESOURCES

Facebook Help, www.facebook.com/help.php, has really good answers to basic questions about Facebook.

Mashable, www.mashable.com, is the blog with the latest and greatest of all things social networking and social media for the person who wants to go beyond the basics.

Progressive Exchange, www.progressiveexchange.org, is a community that shares information among people who organize, market, and raise funds online on behalf of the public interest.

Twitter, www.twitter.com, connects with folks via your computer or cell phone in real time.

Act Now to Win Future Elections

The pundits like to slice and dice our country into red states and blue states; red states for Republicans, blue states for Democrats. But I've got news for them, too. We worship an awesome God in the blue states, and we don't like federal agents poking around in our libraries in the red states. We coach Little League in the blue states and yes, we have gay friends in the red states. There are patriots who opposed the war in Iraq and there are patriots who supported the war in Iraq. We are one people, all of us pledging allegiance to the stars and stripes, all of us defending the United States of America.

—*State Senator Barack Obama,*
Keynote Address, Democratic National Convention,
July 27, 2004, Boston, MA

[45]

Help the Census Count Everybody

At this critical time for our nation, I am grateful that [Robert Groves] will join my team as we take on the challenges American families are facing today. I know that [his] skill, dedication, and commitment to serving the American people will help us move our agenda for the future forward.

—President Barack Obama, on appointment of Robert Groves
to the Director of the Bureau of the Census,
April 2, 2009, Washington DC

THE CHALLENGE

Any organization with an interest in basic civic engagement can help the U.S. Census Bureau make sure everyone is counted as part of the 2010 census.

And if you have any democratic ideals at all, you want everyone to be counted. That includes the people who are the hardest to count—America's disenfranchised.

The more that poor and marginalized people are counted, the more power they have and the more likely it will be that they can work their way out of poverty. It's that simple. For example, if low-income Hispanic citizens are not counted during the census, then the districts in which they live will have less political representation in all levels of government. That's because political districts are created based on the population count of the census.

Also, if low-income populations are not fully counted, they will receive less federal aid, which is often distributed based on census information. So if poor people aren't counted properly, the areas where they live won't get the help they need to battle poverty and gain political clout.

Census workers aren't allowed to talk to the media, but we spoke with one employee whose name we will withhold. He said that, for him, working for the census felt like a continuation of his effort to change America that started when he worked on the Obama campaign. It's all about justice and the equal representation of all people, he said, including the ones who are the most difficult to find. He told us he's looking forward to scouring his assigned areas for every homeless and marginalized person, and helping to ensure that they get the baseline political representation they deserve.

PRACTICAL INFORMATION

- The census is used to calculate the number of representatives each state sends to the U.S. House of Representatives.

- The population distribution of each state, as determined by the census, will guide how state legislative seats are divided, as well as county and city councils, and other voting districts.

- The census data determines the distribution of hundreds of billions of dollars of federal money.

- During the last census, over 14,000 community groups, faith-based organizations, businesses, schools, and local governments partnered with the U.S. Census Bureau to try to count every resident.

- You are required by law to fill out your census form, and all information on it is confidential, meaning the Census Bureau doesn't share information with police, immigration, the IRS, or anyone.

- The census counts all people living in America, not just citizens. Census workers do not ask about people's legal status, so illegal immigrants as well as those awaiting citizenship are supposed to be counted.

- There are only 10 questions on the 2010 census form, requiring only a few minutes to complete—unlike the lengthy form used in 2000.

WHAT *YOU* CAN DO

Find an organization (neighborhood group, place of worship, any community-based organization) to become a Census Partner. All your organization has to do is fill out a short form that's available from the Census Bureau's "partnership staff" in your region. (Get contact information at http://2010.census .gov/2010census and go to "Partner with us.") Organizational partners can do a lot to help:

- Put information about the census or a link to the Census Bureau's Web site on their own Web site, newsletter, or other communications.

- Provide space to the Census Bureau for community events, trainings, or meetings.

- Recruit volunteers for Census 2010 promotional events.

- Sponsor an event to encourage participation in the census.

- Have their names posted on the Census Bureau's Web site.

- Display or distribute census promotional materials.

Volunteer as an individual. To get involved, contact your area's "Complete Count Committee," which consists of community members appointed via high-ranking community leaders. To reach this committee (which may still need members), contact the mayor's office or the county commissioner.

Join the census' "partnership staff" in your region. (Get contact information at http://2010.census.gov.) Census volunteers help staff booths at fairs, parades, or any local event. They might help out at "Questionnaire Assistance Centers," which are set up in libraries and other public spaces where citizens can get help on filling out their census form.

Get businesses involved. Businesses can put census forms on their counter, making it easy for people who lost theirs or didn't get one to fill it out. They can encourage employees to fill out their forms and, more broadly, promote the community organizations listed earlier.

Recruit Census Bureau employees. Workers will be required throughout the process of taking the census. For example, census workers will make six attempts to contact every person who doesn't turn in a form. The Census Bureau needs diverse workers familiar with their different neighborhoods. Individuals, groups, and businesses can help promote possible employment with the Census Bureau.

RECOMMENDED RESOURCES

Leadership Conference on Civil Rights, www.civilrights.org, is a resource for current news, events, reports, and organizations on civil rights and has an effort devoted to the census.

U.S. Census Bureau, www.census.gov/2010census, has lots of information on its Web site, but if you know you want to help, go directly to the page devoted to volunteering: http://2010.census.gov/2010census/more_information/007657.html. You'll also find links to promotional materials, flyers, and fact sheets. To get a form for your business or organization to partner with the U.S. Census, visit http://2010.census.gov/2010census and go to "Partner with us."

[46]

Become a Precinct Captain

Tonight, we are one step closer to that vision of America because of
what you did here in Iowa. And so I'd especially like to thank the
organizers and the precinct captains, the volunteers, and the staff who
made this all possible.

—Senator Barack Obama,
addressing the Iowa Caucus,
January 3, 2008, Des Moines, IA

THE CHALLENGE

"The fact of the matter is, we formed a community," said Hannah
Staub, a volunteer organizer with the Democratic Party. "My goal
was for people to have a good time. So the work wasn't intimidating
for them."

Staub was part of the grassroots uprising that elected President
Obama. But her story started months before the election, before Obama
was nominated, when she started building a base of Democratic voters
that would ultimately help him win. She first organized volunteers to
go door to door, in pairs, on Saturdays, talking with so-called "lazy
Democrats," ones who don't vote regularly. They talked about the
Democratic Party and the upcoming election.

"Our group got to know each other," she said. "We had food. People
became more than acquaintances, and that's continued over time."

But getting people involved wasn't easy, especially early on. E-mails almost never worked to recruit volunteers, even if they were active Democrats, and neither did phone messages. Staub had to talk to a real person. Later, she and other volunteers recruited people as they canvassed.

Staub was a volunteer organizer for a handful of counties. Every county in America is divided into precincts, each of which usually has no more than 1,000 residents. For example, our state's Democratic Party organization has paid staff members who coordinate volunteers throughout the state. There's usually a volunteer "county Democratic chair" who works with the precinct captains in his or her county. And the precinct captain organizes the activities, including the volunteers, in that precinct. Ditto for Republicans in many states.

Think of the precinct captain as the chair of a committee in charge of getting people to vote for his or her party in a slice of your county, the size of which depends on the population density of your county.

Staub's group built lists and identified voters in a number of precincts. Her group later started talking to less receptive but equally important swing voters—a task that some volunteers didn't like. So Staub put them to work elsewhere.

The Democratic community that Staub formed is still active, and building the base of support hasn't stopped. But Staub told us that now the group has changed its focus a bit.

"What we're doing in our region is we are taking seriously Obama's call for community service," she said. "We've taken that to heart here by working at food banks and helping in the community."

PRACTICAL INFORMATION

- Your state political organization is a hierarchy, mostly of volunteers, with the state chairperson at the top. This person is elected, probably by the volunteer county chairs, who are probably elected themselves. The precinct captains may be elected or appointed, with the dominant criterion often being their willingness to volunteer for the job.

- A benefit of getting involved with your state political party is that you get to influence the party. You can vote for party leaders who reflect your political views. And the leadership of the state political party has a major, but not controlling, impact on the candidates who ultimately run for elected office in your state.

WHAT *YOU* CAN DO

Connect with your state political party. For Democrats, visit the Democratic National Committee's Web site (www.dnc.org) and click on "local" at the top. (For Republicans, go to www.gopcom.) Then click on your state and call the office at the number provided. You can send an e-mail, but the phone is often faster, and the president needs your help sooner rather than later. You can also visit www.grassrootsdemocrats.com/new/stateinfo. If you are progressive but affiliated with a different political party, there are similar opportunities there too.

Find out what your local political party needs. Your state political party headquarters will probably refer you to a county chair (explained earlier) or the existing precinct captain in your area. Discuss with them how you can help. When is the next precinct or county meeting? Are any volunteer activities planned? You may discover a void, a rat's nest, or a well-oiled machine. Jump in regardless and figure out the lay of the land.

Try one meeting. Don't send a few e-mails and make a few calls and let the idea of volunteering drop. Find at least one meeting to attend, talk to some of the people, and take it from there.

Get help. If you're having trouble navigating the political party apparatus, find someone who's involved at some level in your state and ask to have coffee. If this is not possible, contact someone at one of the organizations listed in the resource section.

Register and affiliate with a political party. Even the simple act of registering to vote and then affiliating with a political party, if you aren't already registered that way, will build the party and make others take it more seriously.

If you want less responsibility or want to learn more about the local politics before committing more time, you can volunteer for political party activities like canvassing, phone calling, or whatever the party has on its plate at the moment.

RECOMMENDED RESOURCES

Democratic National Committee, www.dnc.org, is the national Democratic Party organization. For other political parties, simply use a search engine to find contact information for your state.

Democrats.com, www.democrats.com, is a group of Democrats pushing the party to the left.

Progressive Democrats of America, www.pdamerica.org, is not a Democratic Party organization, but state chapters often work with Democrats.

[47]

Run for Local Office

I wasn't one of these folks who at the age of five said to myself, "I'm going to be a U.S. Senator." The motivation for my work has been more rooted in the need to live up to certain values that my mother, more than anybody, instilled in me, and to figure out how you reconcile those values with a world that is broken apart by class and race and nationality. And so I guess I have on occasions had to push myself or I've been pushed into service, not always because I thought it was fun or that it was preferable to sitting down and watching a ball game, but because I felt it was necessary.

—Senator Barack Obama, "The Path to Power,"
Men's Vogue, *September, 2006*

THE CHALLENGE

We know there are more people out there like President Obama, who aren't gunning to be elected to any office but care a lot about many things and are seriously committed to making the world a better place—or at least their corner of it. Who can blame them for not wanting to run for office, given the nasty attacks? And the fundraising required. And the time away from home.

But lots of people are working overtime and dealing with jobs that have a downside anyway, yet they often don't even consider running for office.

We hope Obama's own path into politics, starting as a community organizer, will encourage more people to test the political waters. We need the best candidates to run for elected office. That's a core requirement of achieving fundamental change.

PRACTICAL INFORMATION

- There are three levels of elected office in America: federal (which includes the president, U.S. Senators, and U.S. Representatives), state (which includes governor, secretary of state, and state legislature), and local (mayors, school board members, county commissioners, and more).

- Qualifications for elected office vary across the country. Run ForOffice.org has information on qualifications for some state offices, but you should check with your state election office.

- You want to win, but running for office can make sense even if you know you'll lose. An insurgent candidate focusing on a single theme can force an entrenched politician to address a key issue. The legitimacy that candidates for public office have, even if they are long shots, gives them a platform to educate people about important issues.

WHAT *YOU* CAN DO

Assess yourself. There isn't a formula that makes a candidate successful other than a commitment to getting elected—which is a serious one. But you should make an honest assessment of your strengths and weaknesses and get the help you need to win. Some people think, for example, that if they are lousy speakers, they can't run. But actually most people can be trained to be decent public speakers.

Select an elected office. The type of office you seek is less important than whether you can be elected. A good leader can be effective in a variety of offices, if he or she can capture the seat. So access demographic information about the voters where you might run, and determine if you have a shot. (One starting point is to purchase information from the "voter file" for your state, which is described by the New Organizing Institute at www.neworganizing.com/wiki/index.php/voter_file.)

Assemble a committee. This is the best way to get started. It's essential to have a small group of advisors who have skills that you don't and whom you trust. If your campaign takes off, you'll get all kinds of help; but to get started, find a group of people who are dedicated to helping you organize and define your campaign and get things done. Your committee can help you write your campaign plan, and then execute it.

If you don't want to run, draft someone else. Progressive Majority has an online tool that makes it easy for you to encourage local progressives whom you think would be good candidates to actually run. See www.draftaprogressive.com or start a Facebook page to encourage a person you support to run. Then share it with other potential supporters to join.

RECOMMENDED RESOURCES

ActBlue, www.actblue.com, is a good resource for you to quickly get your fund-raising program off the ground.

Campaign Boot Camp: Basic Training for Future Leaders (Sausalito, CA: PoliPointPress, 2008) by Christine Pelosi, is an excellent book for those who want to read firsthand what running is all about from the daughter of the Speaker of the House.

Democracy for America, www.democracyforamerica.com/training, offers candidate training.

Emily's List, www.emilyslist.org, is an organization focused in part on recruiting and funding Democratic, female, pro-choice candidates.

Progressive Majority, www.progressivemajority.org, is a great resource for anyone thinking about running for office as a progressive, and offers across-the-board help.

Run for Office, www.runforoffice.org, gives you access to state candidate qualifications and other resources.

White House Project, www.thewhitehouseproject.org, assists women in gaining leadership roles, including positions as elected leaders.

[48]

Volunteer on a Campaign

This campaign drew strength from the not-so-young people who braved the bitter cold and scorching heat to knock on doors of perfect strangers; and from the millions of Americans who volunteered, and organized, and proved that more than two centuries later, a government of the people, by the people, and for the people has not perished from the Earth. This is your victory.

—President-Elect Barack Obama,
election night victory speech,
November 4, 2008, Chicago, IL

THE CHALLENGE

To really appreciate what President Obama meant when he told us on election night that "this is your victory," you have to be part of a political campaign—and taste just the tiniest drop of success. The intensity and humanity of a political campaign, whether it's a simple petition drive or a presidential election, is unforgettable—and you should give it a try. There's so much more to it than a single candidate, a community organizer, or even the political issues at play. It's about the power of collective action and common purpose.

Obama also said that he felt his election marked the return of government for and by the people. There, we have to say, we disagree, because there are so many more campaigns that need to be won. And believe us, those efforts need you.

PRACTICAL INFORMATION

- Campaigns come in various sizes and stripes. It's useful to think of them as focusing on either electing a candidate or advancing an issue. Candidate campaigns include elections for the school board, state legislature, or Congress. An example of an issue campaign is a ballot initiative to raise taxes for early childhood education. Campaigns are formed to support or oppose a ballot initiative.

- Campaign volunteers sometimes don't do the most glamorous work, even though they're busy saving the world. Common tasks include making phone calls, walking door to door to drop off literature and talk to voters, driving voters to the polls, painting signs, collecting signatures, running errands, and getting pizza or sandwiches from the nearby deli, where the staff claims to be on your side. As a general rule, the larger the campaign, the less interesting the work.

- About half of Americans always vote, and about five percent volunteer for political groups, according to the Pew Research Center for the People and the Press. About a quarter of Americans volunteer for a nonprofit organization, according to the Corporation for National and Community Service.

WHAT *YOU* CAN DO

Find a campaign. Campaigns get going long before they're in the news with any regularity. So you need to watch the news closely for information on the formation or launch of campaigns. Local political blogs track this information more closely. Or you can call your local Democratic Party headquarters or knowledgeable friends and ask about opportunities. Find out if President Obama's Organizing for America has an office in your area.

It's fun to get involved early and get to know everybody, but anytime you want to start is fine.

Pick the right campaign. You'll be happiest (and probably more effective) if you volunteer on a campaign that inspires you for whatever reason—maybe because you're crazy about the candidate or care a lot about the issue. The most "important" campaign, like a race for U.S. Senate, might be the wrong place for you if you love the local school board candidate.

Contact the campaign office. Use the phone, not e-mail.

Do what you say you'll do. Just being on time and reliable will make you a five-star volunteer.

Do whatever is needed. Maybe you can fix frozen computers or speak Spanish. Or maybe you hate phone calls. Campaigns, especially large ones, should be able to slot you into tasks you like. But on a campaign, it's all about getting it done. So be absolutely certain to tell campaign honchos about your skills and preferences, even repeatedly, but do whatever's required, to the extent you're able.

Be thick-skinned. Some campaign offices can be a bit disorganized, and staff can be irritable under pressure. Try to stick it out. Win or lose, it's gratifying to commit until the end, but any amount of time helps.

If you're still hesitant, volunteer with a friend. Especially if you've never done it, it can be a bit intimidating to walk into a campaign office. It's easier with a friend and better for the country because the campaign gets both of you.

RECOMMENDED RESOURCES

All Things Democrat, www.allthingsdemocrat.com/pages/jobsvolunteer .php, provides a one-stop resource to link to jobs and volunteer opportunities within the Democratic Party.

Democratic Gain, www.democraticgain.org, is an association of progressive political professionals. It's mostly for paid staffers, offering networking, training opportunities, and more.

Ballot Initiative Strategy Center, www.ballot.org, tracks local and statewide initiatives and petition campaigns in the 25 states that have them. These campaigns are often in need of volunteers fighting to pass an important cause or looking to oppose an effort pushed by the right wing.

Petition Site, www.thepetitionsite.com, allows you to advocate for one of the many causes already developed or to develop your own petition around whatever issue you choose.

[49]

Register New Voters Year-Round

Our biggest problem is the young, the 18–35 group. There's a lot of talk about "black power" among the young but so little action. Today we see hundreds of young blacks talking "black power" and wearing Malcolm X T-shirts, but they don't bother to register and vote. We remind them that Malcolm once made a speech titled "The Ballot or the Bullet" and that today we've got enough bullets in the streets but not enough ballots. All our people must know that politics and voting affects their lives directly.

—*Community Organizer Barack Obama,*
"Project Vote Brings Power to People,"
Chicago Sun Times, *August 11, 1992*

THE CHALLENGE

It seems like there's a register-to-vote frenzy every election season. But getting more people on the registration rolls is too central to the cause of fundamental change to put on the back burner for years at a time. Let's keep the frenzy happening year-round.

It turns out that registering new voters is easy for everyone to do, not just the good folks down at ACORN. You don't have to join a group or even go to a government office to get started. Just a trip to your computer will work, as long as a printer is attached.

If you want President Obama to succeed, consider walking around with voter registration forms in your briefcase or purse, at the ready when you bump into someone talking about injustice, corrupt politicians, homophobia, sexism, or whatever.

Just ask the apathetic or the dispossessed who cross your life whether they are registered to vote. If not, and you're equipped with the forms or information described below, you've been presented with a mini-opportunity to change America. Sign them up.

PRACTICAL INFORMATION

- Registering voters is a nonpartisan act. So any business or nonprofit can do it without violating campaign finance law. Churches can register voters, too.

- North Dakota does not require voter registration at all. Nine states have some form of Election Day voter registration which allows people to register the day of the election at the polls: Idaho, Iowa, Maine, Minnesota, Montana, New Hampshire, North Carolina, Wisconsin, and Wyoming.

- Many people don't like to admit they're not registered to vote, especially to strangers. So be gentle about how you ask them to do so. You might ask if they need any help registering to vote, without asking them directly if they are registered.

WHAT *YOU* CAN DO

Register people on your own with paper voter registration forms. This is a satisfying action, trust us. Citizens can register to vote in most states, with the exception of Wyoming and New Hampshire, by mailing in the national voter registration form. To make copies, just visit the federal Election Assistance Commission

Web site at www.eac.gov/files/voter/nvra_update.pdf. Print pages two through five, which include "Application Instructions" and "Voter Registration Application." Then scroll down in the same document and find your state listed alphabetically. Copy the address for submission of the voter registration application in your state, and write this address on the reverse side of the form in the space provided. Then you're ready to make copies for yourself and friends to carry around and distribute liberally. You can help by submitting the signed and dated forms after people fill them out.

Encourage people to register to vote online. Just send an online message, via e-mail or Facebook or Twitter, to your friends telling them how easy it is to register to vote online and where they can do it (e.g., www.yourvotematters.org). All they have to do is follow the easy steps on the Web site. Also encourage people to forward your e-mail to their friends.

Volunteer with a voter-registration organization. You can find many local organizations that run voter registration drives. For example, some national groups (like the League of Conservation Voters or America Votes) have state chapters.

Convince a business or institution to help register voters. If you have the right connections (or you're willing to ask anyway), convince a nonprofit, business, or church to encourage voter registration by offering voter registration forms to employees and the public (in the lunchroom, by the checkout counter, in the lobby). They can also include links from company Web sites to nonpartisan voter registration Web sites (e.g. League of Women Voters at lwv.org, or CREDO Mobile's www.your votematters.org).

Support voter registration in swing states. Groups like America Votes, USAction, ACORN, and others organize voter-registration drives in swing states. You can support these efforts by donating to these groups—or perhaps going to a swing state for your next vacation and registering voters.

Register people you know. Despite years of effort, one of our nieces still refuses to register. But we raise the question every time we see her, and some day she'll be on the voter rolls.

RECOMMENDED RESOURCES

America Votes, www.americavotes.org, is a coalition of more than 40 progressive groups focusing on voter turnout and registration.

Association of Community Organizations for Reform Now, www.acorn.org, encourages voter engagement, particularly voter registration among low- and moderate-income communities.

CREDO Mobile, www.yourvotematters.org, offers easy voter registration.

League of Women Voters, www.vote411.org/registertovote.php, is a great online registration tool, in Spanish and English.

Project Vote, www.projectvote.org, supports voter participation and engagement among low-income and minority communities. This is the organization through which President Obama, then a community organizer, registered over a 100,000 people in Chicago in 1992.

USAction, www.usaction.org, is a national group with on-the-ground affiliates in most states that helps register voters in low-income and diverse communities.

U.S. Election Assistance Commission, www.eac.gov/voter, provides lots of official voter information, including the national voter registration form, which is located at www.eac.gov/files/voter/nvra_update .pdf.

U.S. Public Interest Research Group, www.uspirg.org, is a federation of state-based groups that helps voters identify consumer, environmental, and other key issues.

Women's Voices. Women Vote, www.wvwv.org, works to improve unmarried women's participation in the electorate and policy process.

[50]

Donate to Causes You Believe In

> Our campaign was not hatched in the halls of Washington—it began
> in the backyards of Des Moines and the living rooms of Concord and
> the front porches of Charleston. It was built by working men and
> women who dug into what little savings they had to give five dollars
> and ten dollars and twenty dollars to the cause.
>
> *—President-Elect Barack Obama,*
> *election night victory speech, Grant Park,*
> *November 4, 2008, Chicago, IL*

THE CHALLENGE

Even the smallest donation to a grassroots organization helps. Try to
imagine hundreds or thousands of other people doing it, too. That's
what you often have to do to keep the faith as you take baby steps to
save the world. Your small donation can help an underdog candidate
gain legitimacy, just as all the small donors helped President Obama.
Or they can help a struggling grassroots organization show foundations
that it has deep support from people whose pockets aren't so deep.

Small donations can have a big impact on politics.

As President Obama put it in a November 2005 speech: "When the
people running Washington are accountable only to the special interests

that fund their campaigns, of course they'll spend your tax dollars with reckless abandon; of course they'll load up bills with pet projects and drive us into deficit with the hope that no one will notice."

If ordinary people give more money, politicians will be more accountable to everyday people, not just the donors who give lots of money. Likewise, grassroots organizations will be less dependent on grants and the agendas of a few major donors.

And you can take donating a step further by fundraising—trying to convince others to give. It's not as hard as you might think.

FROM THE FRONT LINES

My wife and I sacrificed one trip to the movies per month during the campaign in hopes of making a small difference. During the primaries, yes. But especially against the McCain/Palin ticket, we both felt that it was a stark choice, good versus evil, right versus wrong. We wish we could have donated more. The prospect of another Republican administration, especially that one, was just too scary for words."

—*Ron Sunshine, wedding musician.*

PRACTICAL INFORMATION

- You can track the donations to federal candidates and issues on two excellent Web sites: the Center for Responsive Politics, www.opensecrets.org, or Congressional Quarterly's money-line, www.cqmoneyline.org. At the state level, check out the National Institute on Money for State Politics, www .followthemoney.org. You can find out how much money a specific candidate has amassed and from whom. And you can compare the fundraising profiles of competing candidates. This might help you decide whom to give to.

- You can give tax-deductible donations to some organizations that register voters and work on important issues, but contributions to partisan organizations are not. Ask whether or not your donation is tax-deductible.

- Grassroots fund-raising experts will tell you that the place to start your fund-raising campaign is with your friends and family, even if they aren't rich.

WHAT *YOU* CAN DO

Select a candidate or organization. We like to give to candidates and organizations that are emerging and don't yet have access to large donors. (Of course, it's important to give to major candidates as well, for the reasons stated earlier.) ActBlue can help you identify candidates nationally.

If you don't know the candidates or organizations in your area, ask a friend who's more connected to the political scene.

It can be more gratifying to give to a campaign or organization you're a part of, either as a volunteer or adviser.

Set a goal. How much can you give per year? What can you sacrifice? How about that weekly coffee you don't really need?

Recruit others. The online organization ActBlue (listed in the resource section) makes this easy.

Hold a fund-raiser. It can be a house party or a neighborhood concert. We advise focusing on something fun, which is more likely to attract people—and you get to have a good time whether it succeeds or fails. See our chapter, "Throw a House Party for Change."

RECOMMENDED RESOURCES

ActBlue, www.actblue.com, allows you to start fund-raising for a group or candidate within minutes of going on its Web site. So you don't just donate to candidates here, you can also seek contributions of any size. The site also suggests candidates that have momentum.

Change.org, www.change.org, tracks different issues and encourages citizen involvement, including donations, with groups working on them.

Grassroots Institute for Fundraising Training, www.grassrootsfundraising.org, provides all the resources you'll need to start grassroots fund-raising projects for nonprofits and low-budget campaigns.

The Practical Progressive: How to Build a Twenty-First-Century Political Movement, a book by Erica Payne, is an insightful overview of selected organizations that are helping the progressive movement.

State Voices, www.statevoices.org, is a progressive nonprofit organization that links together and supports states in their goal to engage socially responsible citizens in our democratic process. Your donation is tax deductible.

Conclusion

America, in the face of our common dangers, in this winter of our hardship, let us remember these timeless words. With hope and virtue, let us brave once more the icy currents, and endure what storms may come. Let it be said by our children's children that when we were tested, we refused to let this journey end, that we did not turn back, nor did we falter; and with eyes fixed on the horizon and God's grace upon us, we carried forth that great gift of freedom and delivered it safely to future generations.

—President Barack Obama, inaugural speech,
January 20, 2009, Washington DC

Share Your Ideas to
Help Obama Change America

So don't ever forget that this election is not about me, or any candidate.
Don't ever forget that this campaign is about you—about your hopes,
about your dreams, about your struggles, about securing your portion
of the American Dream.

—Senator Barack Obama, addressing
supporters on the night of the North Carolina
Democratic primary, May 6, 2008, Raleigh, NC

THE CHALLENGE

We know there are way more than 50 ways to help President Obama
remake America. This book boils down to this: how can someone who
cares make a difference?

President Obama's election gives us an unbelievable opportunity
to change America. How can we get our country off the couch to get
it done? How can we help the president continue to move people into
the political process?

Our book, in its small way, is meant to help keep President Obama's
inspiration alive. It's meant to motivate activism, in the broadest sense
of the word. It's not the definitive manual on how to help President
Obama succeed. Such a manual doesn't exist. We just want to get you
started. Your own ideas and creativity are what's essential for remaking
America.

The notion of "50 ways" makes for a decent book title, but last we checked, political reality had more than 50 moving parts—plus the numerous pieces that are so entrenched they barely move at all. And besides, with so much transformation happening in the world so fast, the road map is even more unclear. Great ways to help President Obama are probably being devised in response to circumstances that didn't exist when we completed this book.

That's why we want to hear from you.

Visit www.50WaysYouCanHelpObama.com and tell us what you're doing and what others can do. Our Web site will allow us to brainstorm new ideas, discuss the most practical and effective ways to help Obama, and connect with others who care about similar issues and tactics. This book is a work in progress, and as we look for more ideas, we can keep writing it in real time with your help. We're done being the sole authors. See you on our Web site, we hope.

PRACTICAL INFORMATION

- Talk more about solutions. If you're like us, you probably spend a lot of time talking about what President Obama is doing and those who are obstructing him, rather than what we can do to help him. Try to turn everyday conversations, however briefly, away from analysis and vitriol and toward solutions and actions. Send us any new ideas that arise.

- Don't be shy about suggesting actions. We're all busy, and no one is above reproach for not doing enough, so sometimes we find ourselves reluctant to tell our friends and others to do more for the president, whether it be going to a rally, writing a letter to Congress, or any of the actions we've written about in this book. Now is the time for political action, even if you're understandably reluctant. Tell us how this goes.

WHAT *YOU* CAN DO

Let us know what we should add to the 50 Ways in this book. For example, if you've got a tip on how to get young people involved, green your home, host a house party, fix the broken health-care system, or other ideas, share it with us and others.

Upload your ideas directly on our Web site: www.50WaysYou CanHelpObama.com, where you can also join us on Facebook, MySpace, and Twitter.

E-mail us at: Ideas@50WaysYouCanHelpObama.com

Snail Mail To:
50 Ways You Can Help Obama
c/o ProgressNow
1536 Wynkoop Street, #203
Denver, CO 80202
(303) 991-1902 Fax
(303) 991-1900 Phone

Acknowledgments

We are most appreciative of Michael's wife Debbie, who, along with being a dedicated mom, came up with the idea for this book and provided input all along the way.

There are so many people to thank: To Markos Moulitsas Zúniga and Will Rockafellow, who introduced us to our publisher. Both are true progressives in every sense of the word. To Elizabeth Wagley and Dave Rosen, our pro-bono agents, who also are tremendous resources to the progressive movement by spearheading the Progressive Book Club.

To Thomas Bates, Jeff Blum, Robert Borosage, David Brock, Anna Burger, Ben Cohen, Erin Egan, Scott Goodstein, Nathan Henderson-James, Steve Kest, Dave Reed, Josh Silver, David Sirota, Ron Sunshine, Michael Vachon, and Ralph Walsh who shared their experience from the front lines with us.

We appreciate the assistance of Patricia Bauman, Adam Bink, Jacqueline Davis, Barry Fey, Mike Lux, Jim Lyons, Scott Martinez, Vin Ryan, Heather Smith, Kimball Stroud, Phil Villers, Stacy Weinstein, and Michael Zamore, who provided introductions to help with this book.

A special thank you to our ProgressNow board members, past and present: Kim Anderson, Steve Arent, Brad Armstrong, Brooke Banbury, Adrienne Benavidez, Wes Boyd, Denise Cardinal, Martin Collier, Noel Congdon, Pat Cooper, Mark Eddy, Ryan Friedrichs, Rollie Heath, JB Holston, Rob Katz, Rachel Kaygi, Heather Lurie, Awilda Marquez, Susan McCue, Rob McKay, Kimbal Musk, Bruce Oreck, Doug Phelps,

Jared Polis, Deborah Rappaport, Bill Roberts, Jeff Rusnak, Marguerite Salazar, Gail Schoettler, Andy Schultheiss, Adam Solomon, Greg Speed, Anne Summers, Ted Trimpa, Albert Yates, and Joe Zimlich.

To the outstanding team at ProgressNow who deserve the lion's share of the credit for our success: Jen Caltrider, Bobby Clark, Mike Ditto, Alan Franklin, Liz Mosser, and Brittney Wilburn. To Pat Lombardi, Briony Schnee, and John Stanford, who each helped make this book a priority—on short notice.

To the team at PoliPoint Press—Darcy Cohan, Melissa Edeburn, Scott Jordan, and Peter Richardson—who believed in this book from the get-go.

About the Authors

Michael Huttner is the founder and chief executive officer of Progress-Now, a network of state-based online organizations. In 2003, Huttner started ProgressNow in the back of his Denver law firm with his list of 600 e-mail addresses. Now the 12 ProgressNow partner states' combined membership exceeds 2 million individuals.

Before starting ProgressNow, Huttner worked as policy advisor to Governor Roy Romer and he clerked at the White House for the Office of the Counsel to President Clinton.

Huttner and his wife, Debbie, live in Boulder with their three-year-old son Lee and two-year-old daughter Evy.

Jason Salzman is co-founder of Effect Communications, which serves nonprofit organizations and campaigns, and runs the True Spin Conference, a national conference on media relations for progressives.

He's a former media critic for the Rocky Mountain News, and he's the author of *Making the News: A Guide for Activists and Nonprofits*. His articles have been published in the *Christian Science Monitor*, the *Chronicle of Philanthropy*, the *Harvard International Journal on Press/Politics*, the *Los Angeles Times*, *Newsweek*, *Nonprofit World*, *Sierra*, *Utne Reader*, and elsewhere.

He lives with his wife, Anne Button, in Denver, and they have a 12-year-old son, Dylan, who seldom sleeps, and a 9-year-old daughter, Nell, who never stops.

About ProgressNow

Using an advanced Internet advocacy platform, ProgressNow combines civic engagement, earned media, and coalition-building activities to advocate for progressive policies and interests in strategic states throughout the nation. Our proceeds from the sale of this book go entirely to this grassroots organization. Join our efforts at www.progressnow.org.